Foraging
in
Seattle

Cooking with Delicious
Urban Abundance

or

*Some Mildly Fussy Ways
to Prepare
50ish Foraged
Cultivated & Wild Plants
of Seattle*

Cheryl Wheeler

DEDICATION

To dirt.
You are my Prozac.

CONTENTS

ACKNOWLEDGMENTS

This book would not have been possible without the help of many cheerleaders, editors, and testers. Daniel and Susan read the book and offered detailed structural and grammatical feedback, my son Evan dutifully tasted recipes, and James encouraged me to include only inane illustrations rather than realistic ones. Plant guru Arthur checked over my initial plant list and made helpful suggestions. Several members of the Seattle Cookbook Club read and tested the recipes carefully. Kellie and Shub checked my first full draft for culinary sanity, and then adventurous and skilled cooks Ananda, Christina, Connie, Fred, and again Kellie gave me great detailed feedback on recipes that they made and we all tasted together. Raj grudgingly took several excellent professional-quality photos of me foraging in the summer of 2018, one of which became the book cover. Ananda helped me clarify a chutney recipe and offered a soft option for the pan meino. Tom made suggestions on estimating weights, volumes, and other logical details. Erin provided a helpful read-through and enthusiastic support. Sid and Mohsen remotely approved my Indian and Persian dishes, respectively. Even though it is a small piece of work on a hugely broad subject, this help and detailed feedback was critical to its creation. That said, given that I made all the final edits and publishing decisions for this book on my own, I accept that all remaining grammatical, logical, or factual errors are entirely my own—unless they are somehow not—but they are certainly not the fault of any of the fine people above, either!

INTRODUCTION

Even If You Don't Read Introductions, At Least Read This

Important! While absorbing the content of this book, dear readers, you must be fully responsible for educating yourself about plant identification and safety. Many plants in our area are harmless (the majority, in fact), but some will make you sick, while a select few will kill you. Identification should be taken seriously. I could be a jerk and preface this book by saying it is only for experienced folks, but that runs contrary to my interest in sharing knowledge with people of all levels of experience. So, if you are in Seattle and are not sure know how to get started, Seattle Tilth Alliance (seattletilth.org) is a good place to start with identification classes. You may also investigate plant identification events hosted by the Washington Native Plants Society (wnps.org), although their focus is a little more specific than Seattle Tilth Alliance. There are many free local community events to help people identify edibles, too. Keep your eyes peeled by staying in touch with as many local plant and nature-focused organizations as you can tolerate.

Now that we have that out of the way…

Why Am I Writing This?

This is my third *Super Half Mini Tome for Foodies* cookbook project. If you haven't already looked at my other books, *Some of Each* and *Some of These*, perhaps check them out to learn more about where I am coming from. In a nutshell, I am a curiosity-driven novelty seeker. The abundance of delicious, varied food at this amazing point in human history is incredible when you stop to think about it. Due to this abundance, I learned to cook "just for fun" at a young age—something that has been a rarity in human history (although it certainly has become a popular hobby for the wealthy in the last few hundred years, and even more so in the last 50 years).

Aided and abetted by this cultural milieu, I continue to be endlessly curious new possible flavor combinations. Writing about it all has become a great outlet for sharing just a bit of the knowledge I have built up over the years.

How Do I Know About Foraging?

Somehow, I have been interested in foraging since I was very small. I remember tasting plants randomly in my backyard, and on my relatives' farm, perhaps at the age of four of five. How I got the initial idea to eat those plants, which I am pretty sure were chickweed, I am not sure! Still, I do have a clear memory of my great uncle having an old vinyl record called "Eat the Flowers" or something similar, and the cover was a photo of a cute little girl standing in the middle of, and eating, big pink roses. If she could do it, I could, too! How's that for the power of media to influence children, even an innocent little record cover? I recall that roses were terrible tasting when I got a chance to take a bite! Still, I remained curious enough—or stupid enough—to keep going with tasting and experimenting throughout my life.

While my immediate family had no interest whatsoever in foraging, and my childhood could perhaps be best described as a blur of Appalachian-style outdoor roller skating, I eventually made it through college and got a master's degree in international environmental studies. By that time, I was studying wild plant identification and uses, farming, and urban farming seriously. Since graduate school, I studied edible and medicinal plant uses in Thailand, Arizona, Oregon, and now Washington. My interest in foraging also led to studying permaculture design for several years in Seattle. During my permaculture explorations, I tested growing and harvesting different unusual plants and seeds in my garden and others' gardens to make myself familiar with many new flavors.

At the time I am publishing this, to keep myself immersed and current with my interests in plants, I run a small nature-focused walking tour business and organize a local group of about 400 amateur foragers and foraging-curious folks called the Seattle Area Plant Foragers. I also garden in my neighborhood community garden and occasionally volunteer in local permaculture projects.

I am still learning exciting new plants and plant uses all the time. While you might assume that I know a lot because I wrote a book, I think there is always more to learn! In a few more years, I hope I will know much more. I understand that this super half mini-tome, to be realistic, can only represent a very small selection of the tasty delights available in the lovely Seattle area. I therefore apologize in advance for any and all omissions and overlookings.

Wait, So, What Does "Foraging" Mean in This Book?

I'm no purist by any stretch of the imagination! Foraging, to me, means gathering and eating whatever food is available. The foraged items I cook with are *both wild and cultivated plants*. The wild plants are plentiful because they grow easily around Seattle. The cultivated plants are plentiful because they have been planted and then either were forgotten, or got out of control, or both.

Who Are You?

This book is for confidently curious cooks and bakers. If you find yourself awake in the wee hours of the night wondering if X might go together well with Y, then you get up and try it, this book is probably for you. If you get the jitters wondering if you should or shouldn't try a new flavor combination, or whether or not you are going to regret investing in cooking something, I recommend that you start with some of the more straightforward items described in *Foraging Washington: Finding, Identifying and Preparing Edible Wild Foods* by Christopher Nyerges or *Wild Edibles: A Practical Guide to Foraging* by Sergei Boutenko. I also recommend *Nature's Garden* by Samuel Thayer as a solid starting point. Samuel's adorable enthusiasm and careful attention to harvesting detail are not to be missed.

3

Delicious Abundance, Not Survivalism

These recipes are not survive-in-the-woods recipes. These recipes are meant to encourage people in the Seattle area to discover tasty, fresh, and free local foods by incorporating them into innovative, delicious dishes. The objective is to experience deliciousness. Why experience deliciousness rather than merely survive? Be(cause abundance is) here now! Let's live in the present and celebrate abundance. Let us firmly do away with notions of foraged foods being reserved for gulping down uncomfortably under a leaky tarp. Furthermore, you will see that my recipes often have an international bent, and therefore include ingredients you will not find growing around the Seattle area, such as coconut, olive oil, and the like. If you are a self-identified locavore purist, feel free to scoff and steer clear of all this non-local tomfoolery, but if you are a food lover with access to guilt-free non-local ingredients, do join me.

Organization

This book is organized conceptually by type of dish. I thought about organizing it by season, but because there are some things that can be made almost any time, and most people who read cookbooks expect a conceptual organization, I nixed the seasonal idea to reduce your cortisol levels. Instead, I list all the plants by their typical harvest season in this introduction, and then alphabetically at the end of the book. I sporadically mention harvest time tips in most of the recipes. I believe you can take it from there.

Amounts, Weights and Measures

I do not believe in the imperial system, particularly for weighing. Where it matters, such as in most of the baked items here, or for items that can be tricky to get a sense of how much you really need because of awkward volumes, I include weight in grams and approximate volumes (or both). If you haven't already, please find yourself a nice kitchen scale. A good one currently costs about $20 and you will likely use it all the time. Feel free to eyeball things or estimate as you like, but please do remember that has been your approach when you write me a "the recipe didn't work but I didn't follow the recipe!" review online. Sometimes I think I am being unfair with my stubborn interest in the metric system. But let me know if you really feel that counting by 10s is truly more difficult than counting by 16s.

Even so, I admit that I talk about visual measurements in inches. That's because my mind was conditioned to do so, and I bet yours was, too. Sorry about that if you live in a metric-wise country, but thanks for reading this book and let's chat, because I understand how annoying it can be. If all this stresses you out and you just want a rough guideline, remember that 1 inch is approximately the measurement from the top knuckle on your thumb to your thumb tip, assuming you are an average adult. Know that 1 inch = 2.5 cm. And the average pinky fingernail is about 1 cm wide. 'Nuff said.

Good Urban Foraging Guidelines

Here are the key rules:

- Pick only where you are allowed (city parks and other people's property are off-limits unless you have explicit permission).
- Know which plants you are allowed to pick (some plants are flat out illegal to pick).
- Pick the right plant parts to minimize overall damage to the plant and the general community of plants. If you do not know how to do this yet, you are not ready to pick.
- Leave enough for others —animals (including people) may also like to enjoy the same plants.
- Encourage attractive wild edibles on your property, in parks, and community gardens; well-tended wild edibles that do not spread too aggressively, such as mallow and sheep sorrel, in a community garden can be appreciated by local gardeners.
- Avoid harvesting plants grown in contaminated soils (or areas continually/obviously exposed to air pollutants)
- Do not attempt to forage for profit unless you own the land and know exactly what you are doing with your ecosystem.

Substitutions

Almost all of the foraged foods in this book have a commercially available similar plant that will make a fine stunt double if you would like to make a recipe sans foraging. For example, you see a recipe that you like, and it calls for sheep sorrel (*Rumex acetosella*) but you cannot find any. Please feel free to use your imagination and try another green that you enjoy, such as arugula or baby spinach. It will be a tasty dish and perhaps even more to your liking that the foraged version. I have mentioned substitutions where it occurred to me in the recipes, and I have also listed basic substitutions in the plants list following this introduction.

Special Equipment

Foraging is easy. Well, easier than gardening, I think! Archeologists currently posit that 97% of human history has been lived in foraging mode. Not bad for approximately 188,000 years or 5,371 human generations! This is based on current data I am aware of; I am estimating that "humans" have been here for 200,000 years and agriculture has existed 12,000 years, and an average human generation is about 35 years. In any case, the following are a few things you will likely find useful when harvesting and preparing foraged foods.

- Garden gloves
- All-purpose sharp pocket/camping knife for harvesting
- Scissors for smaller-scale harvesting and cleaning up
- A few good, flexible paring knives
- A few hard, hands-free containers or baskets for collecting
- Food mill (a simple hand-crank model is best)
- Food dehydrator (Check your local tool library if possible)
- Very sturdy fine mesh metal sieves of varying sizes
- A variety of large sturdy colanders for rinsing everything
- Large and small bowls, metal and glass, for various kitchen applications
- A variety of heavy-bottomed pots and pans. I use old copper-bottom Revere Ware, inherited from my grandmother, a few fancy CIA sauté pans, and a few cheap/great non-stick pans.

What about Photos and Plant Identification Imagery?

Tired of text? Seeking glossy photos? Below I list great resources for identification. *This modest self-published book cannot include photos due to the crazy high production cost of full color printing*, but you can find lovely seasonal photos of these plants and more by browsing through (and perhaps following, eh?) my Instagram account, @naturedplantours. Yes, there are a few doodled "illustrations" in this book where space was available. These are for comedic visual entertainment, and in a few cases, may be just slightly educational, but are by no means guaranteed to actually be informative.

Resources for Uses and Identification

While I touch on a few gathering techniques in this book, and I include scientific names of all the plants in the recipes to reduce confusion, I have written this book with only occasional commentary on identification. ***This is intentional.*** I expect (nay, *demand*) that you will consult some of the following resources to familiarize yourself with the plants prior to harvesting any of them. Please note that I have not listed them in any particular order, given that I lean toward anarchy from time to time.

Flora of the Pacific Northwest: An Illustrated Manual Second Edition by C. Leo Hitchcock & Arthur Cronquist (2018, University of Washington Press)

This book is the ultimate identification tome used by botanists in the field. I was required to pack the extremely hefty first edition in my overnight backpack when studying plants in the Oregon Cascades. An excellent reference, although not exactly required for you!

Foraging Washington: Finding, Identifying and Preparing Edible Wild Foods by Christopher Nyerges (2017, Falcon Guides)

Probably my current favorite book in terms of overall usefulness. It fits nicely in your backpack and includes most of what you need to know.

Wild Plants of Greater Seattle by Arthur Lee Jacobsen (2001, self-published)

This is an informative, very well-illustrated and charmingly feisty book by a local plant expert. Arthur offers very well thought-out plant information tours in the Seattle area that you can find listed on the calendar section of his website, arthurleej.com.

Plants of the Pacific Northwest Coast –Revised by Jim Pojar and Andy MacKinnon (2016, Lone Pine Publishing)

A comprehensive and authoritative text that should be referenced by anyone interested in Pacific Northwest plants.

Food Plants of Coastal First Peoples by Nancy J. Turner (1995, Royal BC Museum)

An interesting book for focused study of plants used by Pacific Northwest native peoples in British Columbia. Some of the same plants are found in the Seattle area.

Nature's Garden: A Guide to Identifying, Harvesting, and Preparing Edible Wild Plants by Samuel Thayer (2010, Forager's Harvest Press)

An enthusiastic and detailed book about harvesting and preparing edibles (just as the title suggests). The book is not focused on our Seattle area but has great content. I also recommend Samuel Thayer's cute DVD set, *The Forager's Harvest*. It is not exactly spine-tingling entertainment and he does not mention Latin names (which I find troubling!), but it is useful, especially for beginners.

Wild Edibles: A Practical Guide to Foraging with Easy Identification of 60 Edible Plants and 67 Recipes by Sergei Boutenko (2013, North Atlantic Books)

Indeed, a practical guide! Very easy to read and use. It includes simple, healthy recipes as the admirably long and specific subtitle suggests.

The Front Yard Forager: Identifying, Collecting, and Cooking the 30 Most Common Urban Weeds by Melany Vorass Herrera (2013, Skipstone Press)

A useful and inspiring book by another fellow Seattleite. Very good recipes! The layout and black and white photos leave something to be desired, but I am fully aware that I should not complain about visuals since the ones in this book are so minimal.

The Forager's Feast: How to Identify, Gather, and Prepare Wild Edibles by Leda Meredith (2016, Countryman Press)

This good-looking book contains imaginative recipes, photos, and solid how-to information. I think Leda and Melany Vorass Herrera should combine talents to write a sexy book together about Seattle area specific plants and recipes.

There are many more good books on foraging, and more good books seem to get published all the time. Find a few that appeal to you and curl up with (and/or go traipsing about with) them soon.

Online Options for ID and General Info

Remember to look at all the various extension, nonprofit and for-profit websites out there that have to do with plant identification and use! For me, these are constantly changing, based on whatever works best, but here are just a few that I have cross-referenced regularly in the past year:

Plants.sc.egov.usda.gov

Pnwplants.wsu.edu

Ediblewildfood.com

Gardeningknowhow.com

After trying Google reverse image search with spotty success, I have recently tried using some plant identification apps. My favorite app, so far, is called FlowerChecker. For a small fee it connects you with real live botanists with whom you can chat back and forth. I have used it very successfully when I have been stumped by non-native horticultural plants. I do not feel inclined to recommend any other apps at this point, especially since tech changes constantly (heck, maybe FlowerChecker won't even exist anymore by the time this gets printed!), but you have my permission to find and use any app you trust to assist you with plant identifications.

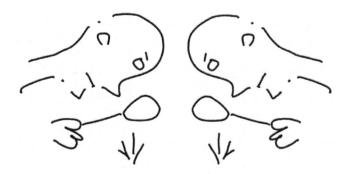

PLANT ID: TWO HEADS ARE BETTER THAN ONE (*MAYBE*)

So, What Plants Are Actually Covered in This Book?

After selecting and testing these recipes, I compiled some goofy charts of the 50ish different items I ended up using or mentioning in the recipes! Some of these items I have just touched on in passing, but these edibles are all available in the Seattle area. Why did I choose these plants? Because I see them when I am out and about in Seattle and have had opportunities to sample them in interesting culinary applications. I am certainly missing many other tasty items—sorry, folks—but they could perhaps be a topic for my next book (hmmm, now let's see). Below I arrange the plants by season. The months are my own idea of what the seasons are in our area. As I mentioned earlier, at the end of the book I have also included a full list of plants, arranged alphabetically.

WINTER (November-February)

Common Name	Latin Name	Parts	Uses	Substitutions
Bittercress	*Cardamine hirsuta*	Leaves	Salad	Mâche, baby spinach or arugula
Chickweed	*Stellaria media*	Leaves	Salad, cooked greens	Mâche, baby spinach or arugula
Common mallow	*Malva sylvestris*	Leaves, seed pods	Smoothie, cooked greens,	Spinach, kale, nettles, gai lan leaves or chard
Dandelion	*Taraxacum officinale*	Leaves, flowers	Salad	Kale, chard, artichokes, broccoli, gai lan
Dwarf mallow	*Malva neglecta*	Leaves, seed pods	Smoothie, cooked greens,	Spinach, kale, gai lan, or chard
Evergreen huckleberries	*Vaccinium ovatum*	Fruits	Fruit, snack	Blueberries
Hawthorn	*Crataegus monogyna*	Fruits (*sans seeds*)	Beverage	Apples, crabapples
Mint	*Mentha spp.*	Leaves	Salad, seasoning herb	Any cultivated mint
Quince	*Cydonia*	Fruits	Savory-sour stew element	Pears or apples, but only minimal so
Rosemary	*Rosmarinus officinalis*	Leaves, flowers	Seasoning	—

11

SPRING (March-June)

Common Name	Latin Name	Parts	Uses	Substitutions
Amaranth	*Amaranthus cruentus*	Leaves	Salad, seeds are a grain	Mâche, baby spinach or arugula
Bay laurel	*Umbellularia californica*	Leaves	Seasoning	—
Chicory	*Cichorium intybus*	Leaves, flowers	Cooked greens, salad	Collards, turnip greens, nettles
Common mallow	*Malva sylvestris*	Leaves, seed pods	Smoothie, cooked greens,	Spinach, kale, nettles, or chard
Daisy	*Bellis perennis*	Whole flower	Salad decor	Any edible flower
Daylily	*Hemerocallis fulva*	Flower buds	Vegetable	String beans, baby okra, asparagus
Dandelion	*Taraxacum officinale*	Leaves, flowers	Salad	Kale, chard, artichokes, broccoli, gai lan, or turnip greens
Douglas fir	*Pseudotsuga menziesii*	New needle growth	Beverage	Citrus peels
Fennel	*Foeniculum vulgare*	Flowers, fruits	Spice	Anise
Field bindweed	*Convolvulus arvensis*	Leaves	Cooked greens	Spinach, kale, nettles, or chard
Grand fir	*Abies grandis*	New needle growth	Beverage	Lemon peels, other citrus peels
Hedge bindweed	*Calystegia sepium*	Leaves	Cooked greens	Spinach, kale, nettles, or chard
Milk thistle	*Silybum marianum*	Stems, leaves	Salad, general vegetable	Kale, collards for leaves; broccoli or gai lan for stems
Lamb's quarters	*Chenopodium album*	Leaves	Salad	Mâche, baby spinach, microgreens
Miner's lettuce	*Claytonia perfoliata*	Leaves	Salad greens	Spinach, arugula, mâche, watercress, other microgreens
Mint	*Mentha spp.*	Leaves	Salad, seasoning herb	Any cultivated mint
Nettle	*Urtica dioica*	Leaves (young ones)	Beverage, cooked greens	Spinach, arugula, mâche, watercress
Ostrich fern	*Matteuccia struthiopteris*	Fiddlehead	Soup, stir-fry	Asparagus (maybe)
Pineapple weed	*Matricaria discoidea*	Leaves and flowers	Beverage	Actual pineapple?
Plantain	*Plantago lanceolata or Plantago major*	Leaves, flower stems	Salad tidbits	Any greens, green beans, asparagus

Common Name	Latin Name	Parts	Uses	Substitutions
Purslane	*Portulaca oleracea*	Leaves	Salad	Tender, thin-skinned green or wax pepper, raw chopped bok choy stems
Red clover	*Trifolium pratense*	All parts	Salad, soup	Spinach, arugula, mâche, watercress
Rosemary	*Rosmarinus officinalis*	Leaves, flowers	Seasoning	—
Sheep sorrel	*Rumex acetosella*	Leaves	Salad greens	Spinach, arugula, mâche, watercress
Sow thistle	*Sonchus oleraceus*	Stems, leaves	Salad	Kale, collards for leaves; broccoli or gai lan for stems
Violet	*Viola spp.*	Flowers	Candy	Any edible flower
Western hemlock	*Tsuga heterophylla*	New needle growth	Beverage	Lemon peels, other citrus
White clover	*Trifolium repens*	All parts	Salad, soup	Spinach, arugula, mâche, watercress
Wild carrot	*Daucus carota*	Flowers	Snack	Carrot

SUMMER (July-September)

Common Name	Latin Name	Parts	Uses	Substitutions
Amaranth	*Amaranthus cruentus*	Leaves	Salad, seeds are a grain	Spinach, arugula, mâche, watercress, other microgreens
Apple	*Malus domestica*	Fruit	Fruit	Pears, crabapples
Black nightshade	*Solanum nigrum*	Fruit (be very careful - completely ripe and black)	Fruit or "vegetable"	Cherry tomato
Blackberry	*Rubus armeniacus*	Leaves, fruits	Beverage, dessert	Any large berry such as raspberry
Blueberries	*Vaccinium*	Fruits	Yumminess	Any small berry such as huckleberries
Burdock	*Arctium minus*	Roots	Stir fry vegetable	firm white sweet potato
Cattail	*Typha latifolia*	Pollen (most parts edible)	Flour for pancakes	Nut meal (hazelnut, almond)
Cornelian cherry	*Cornus mas*	Fruit	Beverage, jam	Tart pie cherries
Dandelion	*Taraxacum officinale*	Leaves, flowers	Salad	Kale, chard, artichokes, broccoli, gai lan, or turnip greens
Goumi	*Elaeagnus multiflora*	Fruit	Salad	Pomegranate
Hawthorn	*Crataegus monogyna*	Fruits (*sans* seeds)	Beverage	Apples, crabapples
Hazelnuts	*Corylus cornuta*	Nuts	Various	Almonds
Italian plum	*Prunus domestica*	Fruit	Dessert	Any plum, apricots
Korean dogwood	*Cornus kousa*	Fruit	Jam, snack	Peaches
Nasturtium	*Tropaeolum*	Flowers, seed pods	Salad, condiment	Capers, other edible flowers
Plantain	*Plantago lanceolata* or *Plantago major*	Leaves, flower stems	Salad tidbits	Any greens, green beans, asparagus
Salal	*Gaultheria shallon*	Fruit	Fruit	Blueberries, huckleberries

AUTUMN (October-November)

Common Name	Latin Name	Parts	Uses	Substitutions
Chickweed	*Stellaria media*	Leaves	Salad, cooked greens	Mâche, baby spinach, or arugula
Common mallow	*Malva sylvestris*	Leaves, seed pods	Smoothie, cooked greens	Spinach, kale, nettles, or chard
Crabapples, apples	*Malus domestica*	Fruits	Snack, condiment	Apples
Dwarf mallow	*Malva neglecta*	Leaves, seed pods	Greens, dolmeh wraps	Spinach, kale, nettles, or chard
Evergreen huckleberries	*Vaccinium ovatum*	Fruits	Dessert, snack	Blueberries
Fennel	*Foeniculum vulgare*	Flowers, fruits	Spice	Anise
Hawthorn	*Crataegus monogyna*	Fruits (*sans seeds*)	Beverage	Apples, crabapples
Mint	*Mentha spp.*	Leaves	Salad, seasoning herb	Any cultivated mint
Nettle	*Urtica dioica*	Leaves (young ones)	Beverage, cooked greens	Spinach, arugula, mâche, watercress
Pineapple weed	*Matricaria discoidea*	Leaves and flowers	Beverage	Actual pineapple (?)
Plantain	*Plantago lanceolata* or *Plantago major*	Leaves, flower stems	Salad tidbits	Any greens, green beans, asparagus
Purslane	*Portulaca oleracea*	Leaves	Salad	Tender, thin-skinned green or wax pepper, raw chopped bok choy stems
Quince	*Cydonia*	Fruits	Savory-sour stew element	Pears or apples, but only marginally so
Rose	*Rosa spp.*	Petals, hips	Beverage, candy	—
Rosemary	*Rosmarinus officinalis*	Leaves, flowers	Seasoning	—
Sheep sorrel	*Rumex acetosella*	Leaves	Salad greens	Spinach, arugula, mâche, watercress

MIND-CLEANSING "ART" BREAK

BEVERAGES

Most of these beverages are very easy to prepare. I have ordered them from easy to difficult, although I think that beverages are already the easiest items you will find in this book.

It might not need to be mentioned, but when preparing drinks, make sure everything you put into the drink is as clean as possible. For example, with the Snotty Mallow Shake, since *Malva neglecta* can grow close to the ground, be extra sure your leaves are as clean as possible. Several bold swishes in a couple bowls of water should be enough cleaning.

You can use other plants to make teas using the same methods I mention here. Nettle (*Urtica dioica*) seems to always be a very popular tea choice. I recommend making tea from common hawthorn (*Crataegus monogyna**) fruit, and the invasive Himalayan blackberry (*Rubus armeniacus*) leaves. Since these two plants are considered noxious weeds in Washington, picking and using them in quantity is very unlikely to be frowned upon by anyone. Another lesser-known but good plant, pineapple weed (*Matricaria discoidea*), which loves sidewalk cracks and lawns, also makes a tasty (vaguely pineapple-flavored!), tea.

I am jazzed to share the cornelian cherry sherbet recipe with you in this section. While this fruit isn't incredibly popular in Seattle, when you do find it, you will see that only a few people are aware of its edibility. You could easily be quite delighted by how productive and prolific the trees are. Its interesting history and popularly in the Middle East may even lead you down the primrose path of food anthropology if you lean in that direction.

Elderflower cordial, an exciting option in this section, has a variety of applications. Get experimental with it! If you are not sure you will like it, IKEA sells little boxes of elderflower drink in its cafes. Based on my extremely limited knowledge of you and your taste preferences, I am pretty sure you are going to like it. I am always surprised that elderflower isn't more popular in the US.

*Hawthorns have poisonous seeds, like apples— but do not fret— just avoid eating the seeds! If this seems perplexing, consider studying your current apple-eating techniques and the fact that you are extremely unlikely to accidently consume the number of such seeds required to kill an average adult.

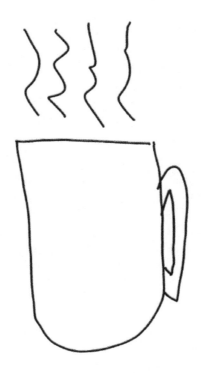

CECI N'EST PAS UNE TASSE DE THÉ

Rose Hip Tea

It is worth questing around for good rose hips. Rose varieties Latin names all begin with *Rosa* and they are all edible. But some are *vastly* tastier than others. You want to find ones that have some hefty flesh around their seeds rather than just a bunch of seeds encased in a thin shell. I seem to find the best rose hips around the month of October, but some are ready earlier or later—keep an eye peeled. Choose hips that are going soft but aren't rotten or moldy yet. Inspect carefully to make sure! I have read that this tea may reduce anxiety, so try it at night—but maybe not so much that it makes you pee all night long, which, speaking from personal experience, is likely to increase your anxiety.

INGREDIENTS

14-15 rose hips, cut in quarters
2 cups boiling hot water

DIRECTIONS

Pour the hot water over the hips. Let it sit as long as you like (10 minutes is about right). Strain out the bits of hips with a strainer and enjoy warm or cool. You can add sugar or honey if you want.

Maybe I should have said this makes just two cups, but I think that's obvious. Adjust proportions accordingly if you want more or less.

Spring Time Fir Tea

The word on the trail is that Douglas fir, *Pseudotsuga menziesii*, is good for you. It is full of Vitamin C and A. It is supposedly good if you are suffering from congestion and is thought to improve immunity. Make this tea in spring when the tips of the trees have the light/bright bits on them that are up to about 1 inch long. Use only those bright green tips—they are very plentiful as well as easy to pinch off. I sometimes eat the tangy bits as a snack while out walking for a "bracing oral experience."

Feel free to apply the same tea concept to Grand fir (*Abies grandis*) and Western hemlock (*Tsuga heterophylla*) when you come across them! Tangent alert: If you have time, look up recipes for fir sorbet, too. Highly recommended by Seattle Cookbook Club folks. Yum!

INGREDIENTS

1 cup of fresh Douglas fir needles — just the bright green tips
2 cups boiling hot water

DIRECTIONS

Mild Option:
Pour the hot water over the fir needles. Let it sit as long as you like (the longer the better for me). Strain out the needles with a strainer and enjoy warm or cool. You can add sugar, or honey, but to feel like a badass, resist.
Intense Option:
Drop the needles in the boiling water and simmer gently for up to 20 minutes. Let cool for 10-20 minutes. Again, you can add sugar or honey, depending on your preferences.

Snotty Mallow Shake

Malva neglecta and *Malva sylvestris* leaves are very nutritious! I always feel awesome when I eat mallows (usually stir-fried). But here you can enjoy their chard-like flavor in an easy smoothie form. Be sure to use a very good high-powered blender to get the leaves really liquefied. From my experience, mallows are good from October through December, but I still see them around at other times. This is a basic recipe. If you taste it and feel like it needs yogurt or whey or mountain oysters or whatever, go for it, and make other additions to your preference.

INGREDIENTS

1 cup packed fresh mallow leaves and flowers (no stems), chopped
1 cup frozen blueberries (or a combination of frozen raspberries, salal, and blueberries)*
Water just to cover all (just enough to allow blending)

DIRECTIONS

Whir all that jazz in a blender very well. Add some salt and honey if you would like to intensify the flavor.

*Are you feeling spartan? If you prefer to taste the mallow more, perhaps use a very mild-flavored frozen melon instead of berries.

Cornelian Cherry Sherbet

Sherbet is a Turkish drink, not to be confused with sorbet or "sherbert" (that's not the correct spelling, anyway)! Sherbet is something hospitable to serve to guests. Cornelian cherry is the fruit of a variety of dogwood tree called *Cornus mas*. It is ripe in the Seattle area in late summer and early fall. Cornelian cherry fruit are deliciously tart and can be frustrating to fully pit, so this is a nice way to enjoy their flavor with minimal effort. This fruit is grown commercially in the Middle East and throughout eastern Europe.

INGREDIENTS

1 kilo (≈7 cups) very ripe cornelian cherries
500 grams white sugar (or no sugar, and sweeten with stevia later)
3 liters (≈12 cups) water

Optional but cute: lemon wedges

DIRECTIONS

Put all ingredients in a big pot and bring to a boil. When it boils, turn down the heat and let it simmer about 20 minutes. Cool on the stovetop. Mash and stir a bit, strain out the fruits and pits, and let the red liquid cool in the fridge for at least a few hours. Serve cold, with some lemon wedges for pizazz.

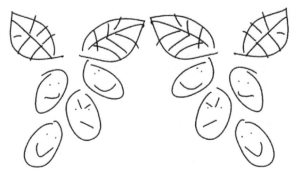

CORNELIAN CHERRY STAND-OFF

Elderflower Cordial

Sambucus canadensis is our wild local variety of elder but you are perhaps more likely to come across *Sambucus nigra*, the European import, which is grown in gardens around Seattle. Elderflowers have a refreshing, light taste. It is well appreciated in northern Europe but sadly much less so in the US. Elders can be a little hard to identify initially because they can be confused with a few other similar shrubs. It is important to know that *only* the flowers and berries (sans seeds—although *cooked* seeds are OK) are considered edible — stems, leaves, roots are toxic and will send you to the toilet for an unhappy moment if ingested in quantity.

You can drink this cordial as part of a cocktail, use it to flavor a cake,* or drink alone over a lot of ice.

INGREDIENTS

3¼ cups water
1250 grams white sugar (yes, that's 1¼ kilo!)
1 large lemon
10-15 fresh elderflowers, blooms only (absolutely no stems!)
3 tablespoons lemon juice

DIRECTIONS

Put the sugar and water in a large saucepan. Heat on medium heat to fully dissolve the sugar, stirring until the liquid is clear. Keep barely warm on very low heat while you do the next two steps.

Slice all the zest from the lemon using a very sharp knife, then slice the lemon innards into fat rounds.

Wash the elderflowers gently in a large bowl of water and shake off the water.

Bring the sugar syrup to a boil, then turn off heat. Add the flowers, lemon peel, lemon rounds and lemon juice to the syrup.

Cover pan with a lid and let it sit for 24 hours. Have some sterilized/perfectly clean jars handy for the next step.

After the 24 hours is up, stir well, and then slowly and carefully pour the syrup, through a colander lined with layers of clean cheesecloth or muslin into a large bowl. Be a good citizen of planet earth and compost the flower heads and lemon tidbits.

Carefully pour the strained sugary liquid into the sterilized jars. I usually just use one giant jar for this, but if you are giving this to friends, use a bunch of cute little jars.

The cordial is ready to drink now, but seems to benefit from a little resting before drinking. It can keep for a few weeks. It is possible to preserve further by canning, but I will not bother with proper canning because I will freeze, drink, or give it all away before much time has passed.

Note: Are you crazy lucky and you have a bumper crop of elderflowers on hand and you want to bake something easy but impressive for a special springtime occasion? Try the elderflower pan meino recipe in this book.

Another Note: Thanks for hanging in there with the notes! Apply this same recipe method, except use the plentiful and typically overlooked pineapple weed (*Matricaria discoidea*) sprigs instead of elderflowers. Yum!

*The easiest way to cakeify cordial is to make a yellow sponge cake in an 8- or 9-inch square pan, and when it is still a bit warm, poke well all over with a skinny skewer, and pour the elderflower cordial slowly over the cake until you think you have saturated it well (please use your best judgement).

SAVORY SNACKS & CONDIMENTS

Here we have some savory snacks to enjoy. "Savory" should be its own food group! Savory snacks are not required be just snacks — you can use them as elements of your meals. Just for example, you can chop up the Rosemary Hazelnuts and add to salads. The Wild Carrot Flower Tempura can be one of many different kinds of tempura served at a dinner. Each recipe here takes a little time, but is well worth it in the end. As in the other sections, I have ordered these preparations entirely subjectively from easiest to most challenging.

You will see that this section includes two chutneys. Chutneys are good with everything, but of course usually served with at least rice (or puttu! WTH is puttu? Read my first book, *Some of Each*). Consider making the two kinds of chutney in advance and then fry up the wild carrot flower tempura for a party time snack.

Note that you can apply the same tempura strategy to any large edible flower that is in season. Squash blossoms are a classic example. If you have access to a community garden, ask some gardeners if you can harvest a few of the non-fruiting squash flowers. Experiment freely!

While the pickled nasturtium seed pods appear last in this section, implying that they are somewhat difficult, do not let that dissuade you. These are a great item to add to other dishes (sandwiches, pasta sauce, pizza toppings, etc.) and a little goes a long way. Making them is something worth getting into. If you like to fiddle around in the kitchen (which is why I assume you are reading this book), they are quite entertaining, and their exciting shape is always a great conversation starter—well, at least if you are having a conversation with me.

Roasted Rosemary Hazelnuts

In addition to making use of hazelnuts (*Corylus cornuta*), found in the Seattle area in summer, this recipe also tips its tiny hat to all the prolific rosemary (*Rosmarinus officinalis*) that grows here, too.

INGREDIENTS

300 grams (OK, 2 cups) hazelnuts, blanched,* and well dried†

1 tablespoon mild-flavored honey or maple syrup
2 teaspoons fresh rosemary, chopped as small as possible
1 teaspoon cayenne powder (optional)
kosher salt to taste (could be a *lot*—just go for it!)
A bit of oil for your baking sheet

DIRECTIONS

Preheat oven to 325° F. In a comfortably sized bowl, mix together the hazelnuts and honey. Sprinkle on the rest of the ingredients. Oil a baking sheet and spread the nuts on the sheet in a single layer.

Pop in the oven for 10 minutes. Stir. Rotate the sheet. Roast another 10 minutes. Stir. Rotate the sheet. Take a good look at the nuts to make sure they do not over-brown. They may need another five to eight minutes. You decide. At the moment they are ready, they will smell good, and they will have turned golden brown but will not have darkened too much. It can be a delicate turning point.

Remove from the oven and leave on the cookie sheet to cool. Sprinkle with significantly more salt. When completely cool, you can put them in a container. I usually put a few of those scary silica gel packets from vitamin jars in the container with the nuts so can resist getting soggy. I have never left them in this state for longer than 4 days before eating them up.

Top secret non-secret: Do not get too worked up about foraging hazelnuts. It is highly likely that the squirrels will get to the hazelnuts before you do, because they check them constantly—think of the squirrels carefully checking the nuts in *Charlie and the Chocolate Factory*. This recipe can also be applied to any other nuts you enjoy whenever the squirrels beat you to the hazelnut punch.

*The best method for removing hazelnut skins is blanching, which means boil the nuts with baking soda, so the skins slip completely off. Blanching means the nut does not get cooked through in the process (as they would if you roasted them, the other popular method for removing skins). You can find the blanching method explained in various places. A nice description of this process is found in a 2016 post on a blog I came across called *Will Cook for Friends*. Do check it out.

†Did you get too excited and you used freshly blanched slightly wet nuts, so now they are sticky even when browned? For shame. Well, you can let the nuts cool and then put them back in the oven on a fresh piece of aluminum foil at 200° F for about 30 minutes to dry them out without burning them. At least this has worked for me in such moments of impatience.

HONORARY CORYLUS CORNUTA PHD RECEPIENT

Random Berry Chutney

If you are a fan of Indian food, as I am, here is a good way to use that random assortment of berries you have discovered during the summer. This recipe is good for using up sour berries because it is based on a traditional gooseberry chutney. The final flavor should be spicy and complicated. Freeze in small containers if you want it to last. The spice amounts can be adjusted to taste.

INGREDIENTS

250 grams random combination of late-summer berries (*Gaultheria shallon* and *Rubus armeniacus* are most plentiful but *Ribes nigrum, Vaccinium parvifolium,* and *Ribes uva-crispa* are good and provide good texture variety)

2 tablespoons canola oil
1 teaspoon black mustard seeds
½ teaspoon yellow mustard seeds
½ teaspoon cumin seeds
1 clove garlic, finely chopped
1-inch piece ginger, grated
2 teaspoons laal mirch (Kashmiri chili powder)*
1½-2 teaspoons salt
1-2 tablespoons apple cider vinegar, lemon or lime juice
2 tablespoons jaggery or brown sugar (plus 2-3 more to taste)

DIRECTIONS

Cook the fruit to soften it completely. You can do this in the microwave or on the stovetop. You do want to do this step to get the fruit to a more jam-like consistency. Press it through a sieve if you want to get rid of the seeds, but it isn't necessary. Drain off any juice (into a glass to drink!) if it seems excessively juicy.

Next heat the canola oil in a frying pan to medium heat, and add the mustard seeds and cumin seeds. Have a lid nearby to cover the pan because the seeds will pop out of the pan.

Throw in the garlic and ginger when the seeds pop and cover with a lid. Jiggle pan momentarily with the lid on it to stir. Take off the heat, then stir salt and Kashmiri chili powder into the oil.

Next stir in the fruit, then the apple cider vinegar or lemon or lime juice. Taste again and adjust seasonings if you want (perhaps more salt and quite a bit of jaggery would be appropriate). Taste. Cook on low heat, stirring, for up to 10 minutes to get the mixture to a good viscosity (my preferred viscosity is a tad more jam-like than runny). You may need to add a little water, just to keep it from scorching; be judicious with the amount.

Serve with whatever suits your fancy in the moment. In addition to eating with puttu, I like chutney as a condiment for Singapore Style Curry Puffs (see my second book *Some of These!*) or Mostly Peas Samosas (see my first book, *Some of Each!*). Seattle Cookbook Club members have also recommend trying it with pork.

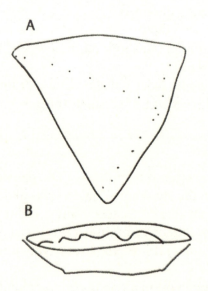

PROTOCOL: DIP A (SAMOSA) INTO B (CHUTNEY)

Kashmiri Crabapple and Quince Chutney

Crabapples are essentially any apple (*Malus domestica*) that is smaller than two inches. They are typically sour. You can use only crabapples if you want. Do not bother peeling crabapples. Can you imagine how tedious it would be? The combination of quince (*Cydonia oblonga*) with the crabapples makes preparing this much less tedious because the quince fruits are big and meaty. Late October, when both fruits are ready, is the best time to attempt this. This chutney is sweet and spicy with a neat color. It makes a nice autumn time gift. Adjust the spices up/down to taste.

INGREDIENTS

500 grams crabapples, seeded and unpeeled, cut into small pieces
500 grams quince, seeded and peeled, cut into thin, small pieces

2 tablespoons unsalted butter
1 teaspoon coriander, crushed
1 teaspoon cumin, crushed
1 teaspoon fennel seeds, crushed

¼ teaspoon ground cardamom
⅛ teaspoon freshly grated nutmeg
¼ teaspoon ground cinnamon
1½ teaspoon cayenne powder
½ cup apple juice (water is OK)
1-2 tablespoons apple cider vinegar

Where to buy spices?
-PCC Natural Markets
-Any Asian Grocery
-World Spice Merchants
-The Internet!!??

½ cup grated jaggery or dark brown sugar
½ teaspoon kosher salt

½ cup finely chopped raw nuts (I prefer half walnuts, half pecans)

DIRECTIONS

Heat the butter in a large, wide saucepan over medium heat. Add the coriander, cumin and fennel and fry. It will smell great as the seeds cook. When it smells great, add the chopped fruit, apple juice or water, and vinegar. Cover and heat to a boil. You want the fruit to get soft. You will need to add water periodically to steam it along. When fruit is cooked, add the powdered spices, salt and brown sugar stir, and let the sugar melt well. Reduce the heat to low and stir. Cook on low heat for about 30 minutes, checking frequently and adding touches of water to prevent sticking. It should become shiny and thick and develop a pink color from the quince.

Turn off the heat, add the nuts, and let the mixture cool completely. Spoon into a variety of perfectly clean, sterilized jars. Cool, then refrigerate. It tastes better after sitting in its jar overnight. I would eat this within a week or so with flaky roti paratha or anything else you think would be yummy! It is a fine idea to freeze this as you would a freezer jam.

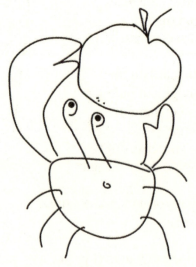

UNAVOIDABLE BAD PUN

Wild Carrot Flower Tempura

What isn't delicious when dipped in batter and deep-fried? Be sure to pick *only* Daucus carota flowers. Since some deadly plants look like *Daucus carota* to the untrained eye, please be more than 100% sure that what you pick are the flowers you want. *Daucus carota* will smell unquestionably good and carroty. If in *any* doubt, try this recipe with some confirmed carrot flowers from a community garden. Note that if you use wet flowers, this recipe will not work, so do not wash them—just dust them well to make sure they are bug free (or leave the bugs on for a mini-protein blast).

INGREDIENTS

142 ounces unbleached cake flour
142 ounces white rice flour

6 cups rice bran oil (or other deep-frying oil of your choice)

1 large egg, beaten
1½ cups cold seltzer water
½ cup unflavored vodka
Ice

≈40 *Daucus carota* flowers

Kosher salt
Hot sauce, chutney, or lemon juice, for noshing

Special equipment: hungry friends

DIRECTIONS

Whisk the cake flour and rice flour together in a medium glass bowl and divide mixture in half. Set aside. Heat the vegetable oil in a very heavy 5-quart pot over medium-high heat. Your target is 375° F on a top quality deep-fry thermometer, but your next step starts at 365° F.

Once the oil temperature reaches about 365° F, whisk the egg, seltzer water and vodka in a medium mixing bowl. Divide it in half such that half of the mixture can go into the refrigerator to maintain its bubbliness and you can pour the other half of the liquid mixture into half of the flour mixture. Whisk to combine, about 10 to 15 seconds. Some lumps may remain, but do not over stir.

Set the batter-filled bowl in a larger bowl lined with ice. Dip the flowers one by one into the cold batter using good quality tongs or chopsticks and drain for 2 to 3 seconds over the bowl, and then gently baptize them in the 365° F oil.

Maintain the oil temperature between 365 and 375° F. Fry only a few pieces at a time, until puffy and very light golden.

Remove flowers to a cooling rack lined with 3-4 layers of paper towels set over a half sheet pan. Sprinkle generously with salt.

When you run out of batter, mix up the set aside halves and keep going!

Serve the tempura as it is made, immediately, with hot sauce, chutney, fresh lemon juice, or anything else that tickles your fancy.

It is generally said that tempura may be kept in a 200° F oven in a single layer for up to 30 minutes on a baking rack set inside a sheet pan, but they are best when eaten immediately.

Secret note: Does this recipe sound tedious? Why not make use of a little leftover pancake batter and dip the flowers in that, then fry in a generous amount of oil in a shallow pan like flower-filled funnel cakes? I tried this right after I read about it while researching fried flowers recipes, and it was fairly decent. Like all deep-fried things, success with this approach depends largely on how you manage your timing and overall oil temperature!

Pickled Nasturtium Seed Pods

This is a multi-day recipe and a little goes a long way, so you will have plenty to use later! I think of these seed pods as extra-large "triple capers." I like to add them to salads, salad dressing, egg salad sandwiches, spaghetti and put a bit in pizza sauce or on a pizza.

Nasturtium is a commonly grown annual garden plant with spicy tasting bright orange and yellow flowers, and its Latin name is *Tropaeolum*. It is not closely related to the *Nasturtium* genus, which is watercress (*Nasturtium officinale*)*. The seed pods appear toward the end of summer when the flowers are wrapping up.

INGREDIENTS

Tropaeolum Thruple

1⅓ cup fresh nasturtium (*Tropaeolum*) seed pods
½ cup kosher salt
4 cups water
⅔ cup white vinegar
1-2 teaspoons sugar
Small dried bay leaves†

DIRECTIONS

Snip nasturtium seed pods from their stems. Choose only the ones that look and feel crisp. Rinse well and dry between layers of fluffy kitchen towels.

In a large glass jar, stir together salt and water. Stir in the nasturtium pods, then find a way to keep the pods submerged. I do this by putting a big shot glass into the jar just so, but I have read you can use a plastic zip-top bag that you push into the salt water just far enough so the pods will not surface.

Rest the jar at room temperature for two days. The pods will darken and now look more caper-y by the end of the second day.

Dump the pods into a strainer and rinse off the salt. Next, boil your vinegar and sugar in a small saucepan. Stir so the sugar dissolves.

Divide your pods into small, adorable jars to your liking, then pour the hot vinegar over the pods, covering them completely. Now you may attractively place a small, dry bay leaf into the side of each jar like a wacky foodie calling card.

Let cool, then put on the jar lids. Keep in the fridge or not. The pods will stay preserved for a long time.

Note: Bonus surprise! You can follow this same process for *Malva neglecta* fruit pods (they look like adorable little magical pumpkins, but many people describe them as "cheeses") if you do not mind taking the time. And if you have time to look it up, find out what Pliny the Elder said about *Malva neglecta* seeds—fun times!

Super Bonus Surprise Note: But wait! You can also use this same recipe to pickle sow thistle (*Sonchus oleraceus*) flower buds and use them in all the same ways. Interesting, isn't it?

*Although both plants are edible in this case, these kinds of issues with common names are even more reason to always use Latin names when cross-checking and verifying plant identities.

†Bay, or bay laurel (*Umbellularia californica* is our local west coast variety), grows forgotten all around Seattle in many people's lawns and gardens. It has some non-edible vaguely similar look-alikes, so get to know some bay laurel shrubs in your area. If you hanker for the tiniest, prettiest bay leaves, which look adorable as hell in little gift-size jars of pickled nasturtium seed pods, get to know some shrubs and look for the new growth in spring. Dry these tiny leaves under a weight because otherwise they tend to curl up. You will not have any curling issues with big bay leaves— I just toss those in a loose pile in a dish in my kitchen and they eventually dry out flat, or relatively flat enough, in a few days.

SWEET SNACKS

Sweet snacks might be the best way to get yourself and reluctant others turned on to foraged foods. Who doesn't like picking berries and eating cookies, right? While I was editing, I noticed that most of these recipes are baked, or involve an oven, anyway. This has to do with my love of baking, I suppose. My next book is probably going to be titled *Leave Me Alone: I Just Want to Bake This!*

OK, a bit about the recipes. If you enjoy black licorice, you are going to enjoy the fresh fennel cookies. Skip them if you are *not* into licorice. The nutty salal fruit muffins make a good snack or breakfast. The PNW fruit nut bars are a compact snack good for packing along on a hiking excursion. I feel that the sweet crunchy hazelnut chunks and the salal hazelnut biscotti are appropriate tea time treats for holiday guests.

While the cattail pollen pancakes are easy to make, the time it takes to go collect the pollen should be a consideration. The fastest way I have seen to collect cattail pollen seems to be to cut a hole in the side of a plastic gallon milk jug, stick the top of the cattail in the hole, and shake the jug. The pollen flies everywhere, but gradually falls down the sides to the bottom of the jug. This is considerably more efficient than tapping the pollen into a bag, in which case the pollen blows away in the wind (as it is designed to do). I saw the nifty milk jug harvesting technique demonstrated in Samuel Thayer's DVD set, *The Forager's Harvest.*

As with the other sections of the book, I have ordered these recipes generally by what I consider easy to difficult, but it is up to you to determine what is most manageable in your own perceived reality.

Fresh Fennel Cookies

These buttery cookies, made with *Foeniculum vulgare* fruits, have a delicate, sweet fennel (or anise, or black licorice) flavor. The optional orange is a nice compliment, but if you are extremely in love with fennel, it might feel like some unwanted competition, so I will let you decide. Delicious with a good quality black tea!

INGREDIENTS

226.8 grams (OK, 1 cup) room temperature unsalted butter
200 grams white sugar
1 large egg
1 tablespoon chopped fresh fennel fruits,* still green,† finely chopped
1 tablespoon water
200 grams all-purpose flour
¼ teaspoon baking soda
⅛ teaspoon salt

Optional: freshly grated rind of one orange

DIRECTIONS

Cream the soft butter with the sugar until it looks fluffy. Beat in the egg, water, and the finely chopped fresh fennel fruits. Sift together the all-purpose flour, baking soda and salt then mix into the creamed mixture.

When all is well-combined, cover and chill the dough about 30 minutes to firm up the butter a bit. Now you can attempt to shape dough into two long rolls, about 9-10 inches long (longer if you like smaller gauge cookies). Roll the rolls smooth so they are lovely cylinders, or make them rectangular blocks if that feels right to you. Do your best, as the dough is soft—you may want to shape, chill it a few minutes, then work on further shaping until you get them as uniform as you can handle. Wrap in parchment paper, using the

37

paper to guide your shaping. Put in the freezer for much later or in the refrigerator for 1-2 hours if you're hurrying to bake them today.

Whenever you are ready to have some cookies, get the dough out and let it warm up for 10-12 minutes, or until you can cut the cylinders into neat ¼ inch slices (or thinner).

Put the slices on an ungreased cookie sheet about 2 inches apart (they will spread) and bake at 375°F for approximately 12-14 minutes until they are golden around the edges. If you decide to cut them larger, do give them more space as well as more minutes in the oven because they aren't going to be golden yet at the 12-minute mark. Keep an eye on them! Cool on the sheet on a rack for 10-15 minutes before gently moving them to your mouth.

*Technically fruits, not seeds, but they will generally look like "seeds."

†You may also use the fresh yellow fennel flowers because they are very yummy, too, but I recommend doubling the amount.

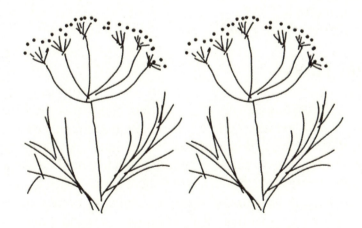

FRIENDLY FENNEL FRONDS 'N' FLOWERS

Cattail Pollen Pancakes

Cattails (*Typha latifolia*) make most of their high-protein pollen during the summer solstice and you can get quite a lot of pollen from them if you pay attention. I think this recipe is the easiest way to use cattails for food— it is tidier than digging or pulling up cattail roots and it feels less violent than chopping off the flower spikes in spring while swamp wading. This makes a small amount—double it if you have more pollen available!

INGREDIENTS

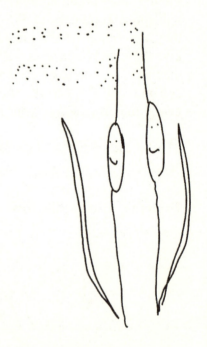

Dry Items
½ cup cattail pollen
¼ cup white whole wheat flour
¼ cup hazelnut or almond meal
1 tablespoon sugar
½ teaspoon baking powder
½ teaspoon kosher salt

Wet Items
1 large egg
1 cup buttermilk
3 tablespoons oil or melted butter

DIRECTIONS

Mix all the dry ingredients together. Separately, mix the wet items together. Stir wet items into dry items. Pour onto a greased medium-hot griddle in small, thin pancakes. Cook until bubbles appear. Flip. Cook until they look and smell edible, which should just be a couple minutes. These are delicate, so treat them gently when flipping and watch carefully for burning. Serve with whatever other yummies you like—maybe try it with my Kashmiri crabapple and quince chutney.

Nutty Salal Fruit Muffins

Good stuff, here— *if* you are into muffins. These are soft, fluffy, high-fruit content, and crumbly. The mini muffin tin makes them into nice little bites. Be sure the bananas are very ripe for maximum natural sweetness and mush. I have occasionally replaced the bananas with mashed cooked white sweet potatoes with interesting (heavier but tasty) results. These muffins happen to be vegan and gluten free, although that is not the main objective. The main objective is to get you to eat salal.

Salal, *Gaultheria shallon*, is a plant that grows everywhere in Seattle in the summer and most people do not even notice it because it is really kinda just *everywhere*. Salal is usually at its best in August when we are distracted by blackberries. Pick and wash your fruit, then make these muffins the same day. I do recommend including the chopped nuts at the end, but I am not offended if you think better of it. If using so many salal berries seems weird to you, try half salal and half huckleberries. Red huckleberries with the blue salal berries make an entertaining color combination.

INGREDIENTS

Dry items
½ cup rolled oats (58 grams)
¼ cup hazelnut meal or almond meal (38 grams)
3 tablespoons flax meal
A few bold strokes of freshly grated nutmeg
Fat pinch of kosher salt
½ teaspoon baking soda

Wet items
¼ cup nut butter of your choice
2 large very ripe bananas (about 340 grams)
2 tablespoons maple syrup, honey, or molasses
1 teaspoon vanilla

Stir in

1 cup freshly picked, washed salal (*Gaultheria shallon*) berries
2-4 tablespoons top quality chopped nuts

DIRECTIONS

Preheat the oven to 375° F. Lovingly lube a 24-seater mini muffin tin for use.

Whir your dry items in a food processor until all is finely ground. Do start with the oats first, though, as you do not want to inadvertently turn the nut meal pasty before the other items are well whirred.

Mash up the wet items well in a large bowl. Stir in the dry items well,* then gently stir in the fruits and nuts.

Spoon batter into the prepared muffin tins, about ¾ up the sides. Bake about 15 minutes but note that depending on your choice of nut butter, sweetener and the size of the bananas, this could be more or less time. If you stick a metal skewer/fork tine/knife in one, it should come out clean. If not, bake a few more minutes and re-probe for doneness.

Let cool about 10-12 minutes, then un-tin and consume! Tasty with my strawberry tree jam!

*Stir as much as you want, you crazy kids! No gluten in this recipe means that over-stirring causing toughness via gluten strand formation will not be an issue.

PNW Fruit-Nut Bars

Initially I thought I should include a hard-core recipe for fruit and salmon pemmican in this book. But pemmican, especially fish pemmican, is, pretty, um, *intense*. It is something you are totally going to love if you are very hungry, so it would taste great! But frankly, as close as we've become over the last 40-odd pages, I know by now that you are not going to go out of your way to make salmon pemmican. At least not today.

So instead I came up with something I consider somewhat pemmicany that you can pack along on for a hike and uses all PNW products. All ingredients are available fresh in summer, but really you can make these any time.

INGREDIENTS

1 cup fresh hazelnuts,* ground into fine crumbs
1 cup dried blueberries, chopped
1 cup dried huckleberries, chopped
1 cup dried salal berries, chopped
¼-½ cup hazelnut butter† (just enough to stick everything together)
Salt (to taste)

DIRECTIONS

Put the hazelnuts in a good food processor to chop very small. Add dried fruits. Whir until well combined but still chunky. Pull out of the food processor, put in a bowl, and start adding nut butter tablespoon by tablespoon to it just until it holds together. Taste. If you want to salt it, do so now, and knead everything together well. It should hold together in a ball fairly easily. Press very firmly into a small pan—I use a small bread loaf pan lined with parchment paper. Next cut into bite-sized squares or rectangles with a sharp knife. Un-pan the pieces (that's why I use the parchment paper—I can just lift them out of the pan with the paper) and freeze individually in wax paper or plastic wrap to pack along on day hikes.

Top secret note: Not going to take the time to dry these fruits yourself? Try this with dried fruit items you buy at the store/market. I promise to not tell anyone.

*Skins on is fine, do not worry about blanching the nuts in this application!

†Substitute another nut butter if you couldn't make or find hazelnut butter. I have tried sunflower seed butter but tastes a bit strong unless you really adore the taste of sunflower seeds. I usually recommend almond or cashew butter when hazelnut butter is elusive.

CLICHÉ FRUIT-NUT BAR MAILBOX PEAK HIKING SELFIE

Sweet Crunchy Hazelnut Chunks

The egg white seems strange initially, but these are quite tasty! Do not attempt this with unblanched hazelnuts—the texture and flavor of the skins is too strong! Good to make any time you have some raw hazelnuts on hand. Chop them just to rough them up. They will be too hard to spread out if you chop them finely. Works great with pecan halves, too.

INGREDIENTS

For every 1 cup blanched and barely chopped hazelnuts:
> ¼ cup sugar
> Good pinch kosher salt
> 1 large egg white, stirred

DIRECTIONS

Generously butter a baking sheet and set the oven to 300° F. Put the sugar and salt in a bowl. Stir together the blanched hazelnuts and egg white with your hands. Make sure they are well coated with egg. Drop the coated nuts into the sugar-salt and coat them thoroughly.

Put the nuts onto the buttered baking sheet so none of them are touching. Bake 30 minutes. Cool on the baking sheet, and when totally cool, stick in a sexy looking bowl or container. Serve as-is, or chopped up on ice cream!

CRUNCH ROCKERS

Elderflower Pan Meino

This is a northern Italian recipe, typically made with corn flour and European elderflowers (*Sambucus nigra*). Sadly, even Italians now leave out the elderflowers because of lack of proximity to the plants. You can make them plain as well, but I think they taste better with some complimentary-tasting plant matter added. For example, I have replaced the flowers with lime zest (two limes worth) before with very tasty results. You can try other flavors of interest to you as well!

INGREDIENTS

100 grams white sugar
100 grams unsalted butter, at room temperature

2 large eggs

150 grams corn flour*
90 grams all-purpose flour
⅛ teaspoon kosher salt

2 teaspoons baking powder
≈¼ cup chopped elderflower blooms, *no* tiny stems

Powdered sugar to top (optional but festive)

DIRECTIONS

Cream sugar and butter together quite well with a hand mixer. Add the eggs and cream together well. Stir in the flowers now to distribute them as thoroughly as possible.

Stir together your dry ingredients, then add all at once to the butter-eggs-flowers. Stir just enough to combine (aim to not over-stir). The dough will be soft, and reasonable to shape when handled gently. †

Form 18-20 balls (if you want them to bake evenly, which is a good idea, weigh the dough and divide it equally). Put them on a parchment or silicone baking mat lined baking sheet, with a couple inches between them. Note that they will puff and spread just a touch—and they are better if they do not run into each other.

Bake at 350°F for 13 (soft!) -18 (crispy!) minutes. When done, they should be a bit cracked open and feel firm, which makes for great biting later. Cool on the sheet pan, on a rack. When they are cool, use a sieve to evenly distribute a touch of powdered sugar over them. This is completely optional but does help fancy them up for a good tea time presentation and falls nicely in the cracks.

*"Fine grind cornmeal" or "corn flour" needs to be on the label. Masa harina, or the regular coarser cornmeal favored by southern folks will not work the same way. Corn flour should not be confused with cornstarch, because cornstarch is called corn flour in Asia. Fun.

†Struggling? Chill dough 10-15 minutes in fridge until it behaves.

UNASSUMING PAN MEINO DELIGHTS

Salal Hazelnut Biscotti

A sneaky way to get you to eat your salal (*Gaultheria shallon*). Your friends will be impressed by the exotic fruit and all your effort. Or they will have no idea and assume that they are eating blueberries. Either way, you win! The salal will be ready during mid to late summer and the hazelnuts will be ready around late August-ish. This is a good recipe for pantry packrats like me because it makes use of items that stick around in preserved form. Substitute any nut or fruit.

INGREDIENTS

1 egg yolk
2 large eggs
200 grams white sugar
1 tablespoon rum

250 grams all-purpose flour
½ teaspoon baking powder
¼ teaspoon kosher salt

100 grams toasted hazelnuts, chopped
½ cup chopped dried salal fruit

DIRECTIONS

Preheat oven to 350° F and line a baking sheet with parchment paper.

In a large bowl, beat eggs and sugar together very thoroughly with the rum. Stir together flour, baking powder, and salt, then add to the eggs and sugar. Stir well, then add hazelnuts and chopped salal. Distribute the nuts and fruit well. The dough should be firm and sticky.

Oil your palms (failure to do so may cause woe)! Grab the dough and on your paper-lined baking sheet, pat the dough into an oblong about 3 inches wide. Try to get a smooth, even shape, but the shape does not need to be totally perfect.

Bake until just light golden and firm (about 25-30 minutes), perhaps rotating the sheet at about 15 minutes to ensure and even bake.

Remove from the oven. Keep oven on but turn it down to 300° F. Let the loaves cool on sheet on a wire rack for 15-20 minutes.

As soon as the loaf is cool enough to cut without breaking apart (20ish minutes), get a good serrated knife and cut the loaf, on a cutting board, as deftly as you can into hearty ¾ inch diagonal (or non-diagonal) slices.

Arrange slices, cut side down, on the baking sheet.

Now you just bake until the slices are crisp and golden, about 30-40 minutes (yes, the ¾ inch slice takes a while to crisp at 300° F). I recommend rotating the sheet and turning each biscotti over at the 15-minute mark to encourage even browning. Finally let the biscotti cool on the sheet on a wire rack. They should store nicely and stay crispy if you baked them to the proper point of dryness. If you are a maniac about maintaining crispness, you can also add a few silica packets from pill bottles to the cookie jar to extend their crispness.

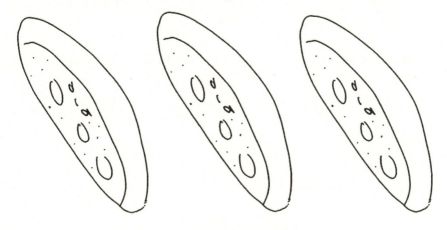

BISCOTTI BEOTCHES

SALADS

Oh, salads. If you have read my other books, you have heard me whine about the tribulations of vegetable prep. Here I shall dip a toe into practicing mindful speech and proclaim that salads are tasty and worth the effort when foraging.

Think of the various documentaries you have watched about foraging in pre-agricultural societies. Thousands, right? Well, I am sure that at some point in these films, you noted that the foragers always went out in groups. Beyond the safety-in-numbers aspect and social pleasures of hanging out with comrades, it is also significantly more practical to forage as a group. You will find a wider variety of items, plus your total results will pile up faster than when you are out bumbling around alone. Additionally, particularly when gathering delicate items, far fewer plants will be smashed due to more people having adequate space in their baskets and bags!

As in the other sections, I have organized recipes from easiest to most challenging, strictly based on my own experiences and opinions. Within the recipes, I have made some suggestions for pairing with other dishes and foods.

I love all these salads, so I won't blather further—just check them out!

Goumi Salad

Goumi (*Elaeagnus multiflora*) are too tiny to seed, so treating them like pomegranates is a great approach when you are tired of languidly eating them directly from the bushes. Goumi are popular with the permaculture crowd and are popping up more and more in community gardens and parks. Around Seattle, I see that goumi are ready to pick through the month of September. Not sure where to pick? The Beacon Food Forest has a huge number of goumi shrubs and thoughtfully welcomes hungry visitors!

INGREDIENTS

Dressing Bits *
2 tablespoons apple juice
1 tablespoon lemon juice
1 teaspoon Dijon mustard
2 teaspoons mayonnaise
2 teaspoons honey
1 tablespoon olive oil

Salad Bits
≈2 cups tender greens† of your preference, torn
1 medium sized yellow apple,†† chopped into bite-size squares
⅓-½ cup whole fresh goumi berries
Freshly ground black pepper, to taste

DIRECTIONS

Shake the dressing ingredients together very well in a small jar with a lid.

Put everything else in a bowl, stir gently with your hands. Pour the dressing over, turn and stir gently with your hands again. Serve immediately!

*Much Apple salad dressing (see next recipe) also works well here.

†Feel free to use sheep sorrel (*Rumex acetosella*), mâche, arugula, or watercress (*Nasturtium officinale*) instead. Or any blend of tender fresh greens from the grocery store will be yummy.

††Firm but ripe pears or Asian pears are great too—as well as some of the larger crabapples. It just depends on what is available.

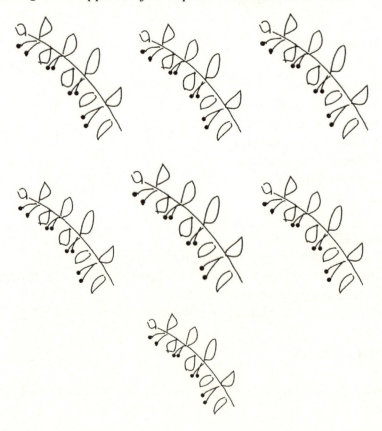

WHENEVER THERE'S TROUBLE, WE'RE THERE ON THE DOUBLE, WE'RE THE GOUMI GANG

Much Apple Salad

Perhaps I risk being a bit obvious with this one, because apples (*Malus domestica*) are super familiar to everyone. But I think it would be a shame to exclude apples from this book because you would not believe how many neighborhood apples go to waste in Seattle every autumn. We are just too overwhelmed; not even the birds, squirrels and any other critters can eat them up.

I say make use of plentiful apples in every possible way. This makes a good size salad for four. Adjust as you prefer.

Side note: City Fruit (check them out at cityfruit.org) harvests excess apples all over Seattle to deliver to food banks and process into cider. Join their volunteer activities to celebrate Seattle fruit abundance.

INGREDIENTS

Dressing Bits
2 tablespoons mild-flavored salad oil of your choice
2 tablespoons mayonnaise
¼ teaspoon kosher salt
2 tablespoons apple cider vinegar

Salad Bits
4 cups apples, any variety you find (a mix of red and yellow is good), chopped in bite-size bits
2-3 tablespoons roasted hazelnuts, chopped
¼ cup dried or fresh salal berries (or dried or fresh blueberries or huckleberries)

2-3 cups tender greens of your choice, torn

DIRECTIONS

Mix the first four items in a jar with a tight lid and shake vigorously to combine into a dressing. Put apples, nuts and berries in a bowl and gently stir in an amount of the dressing that suits you, using your hands. The dressing is runny but sticks well to the salad bits (if you want it less runny, decrease the oil and increase the mayonnaise). Put the lettuce on plates and top with the dressed bits. Consume right away to experience maximum crunchy freshness!

OUTSIDE THE CLUB APPLE BOMB

Quinoa Plantago Salad

Plantains (the two most obvious ones are *Plantago lanceolata* and *Plantago major*) are almost everywhere, extremely hardy, and easy to identify. Why not put them to good use, then? This recipe is tabouli-esque, except it uses quinoa instead of bulgur wheat, and it is meant to be much more vegetables than grains. As with tabouli, be extra sure that all your ingredients, especially your greens, are very dry. The whole dish can end up soggy if you do not dry everything thoroughly. You will be sad if that happens. I specify Sun Gold cherry tomatoes because that is the only variety of tomato I see get ripe and tasty in Seattle with predictability.

Choose leaves that are new shoots, not old and tough. Since (*good*) tomatoes are not ripe until approximately August, and plantago tends to be most tender when it is a newly grown leaf, choose plantago from your yard that has recently been mowed or pinched off at the base such that it has produced tender leaves. Does that sound tedious or not exactly feasible? Substitute tender kale, spinach, or gai lan leaves!

INGREDIENTS

½ cup red quinoa
1 cup Sun Gold cherry tomatoes,* quartered
≈1 packed cup tender *Plantago lanceolate or Plantago major* leaves, very finely chopped
1 bunch flat leaf (Italian) parsley, including stems, washed dried, very finely chopped
15-20 fresh mint† leaves, washed, dried, and very finely chopped
½ small sweet white onion, very finely chopped

Kosher salt to taste
3 tablespoons fresh lemon juice
¼ cup top quality extra virgin olive oil

DIRECTIONS

Rinse the quinoa if needed, then cook in a rice cooker with an appropriate amount of water until soft and edible. Spoon out onto a big plate to get it to cool and let it dry out a bit.

Very finely chop the plantago leaves, parsley, mint and onion. Put chopped tidbits in a large bowl with quinoa. Pour in the lemon juice and olive oil, then stir with a big spoon. Salt generously/to taste to add the tomatoes.

Cover for a bit to let the flavors blend together. 20 minutes is adequate. Transfer to a serving plate or put in the fridge to keep for later. Stays relatively decent for about a day or two.

*If you feel bold, you can replace the cherry tomatoes with the ripe fruit of edible black nightshade, *Solanum nigrum*, but only if you are **absolutely certain** that you have the real *Solanum nigrum* and not a toxic nightshade variety. The immature green fruits of *Solanum nigrum* are poisonous, but the fully ripe black fruits are tasty like tomatoes. Read more about it in Samuel Thayer's *Nature's Garden* as well as in Christopher Nyerges' *Foraging Washington*.

†You can also easily forage mint (*Mentha spp.*) for this dish— it is all over Seattle. Just learn to identify it and you are good to go.

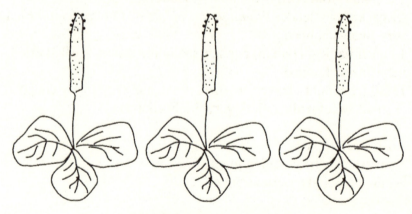

PLANTAGO PATROL

Purslane Leaf Salad

Portulaca oleracea (commonly called purslane) is refreshing, crunchy and a wee tad slimy. The best things in life are slimy. This way of preparing purslane keeps the slime in check. Your novelty-loving friends (such as me—thanks for having me over!) will be ultra excited to see something different on their plates. Purslane is available pretty much all summer and it prefers to grow in rich garden soil. Instead of pulling it out to make room for other vegetables in the garden, give yourself a break from unnecessary effort, relax, and accept purslane as a free, no-effort vegetable!

This salad is very nice alongside some protein, like some (sustainably caught) fish or some skillfully marinated grilled tofu. You can substitute top-quality thin-skinned chopped Hungarian wax peppers for the purslane leaves with tasty results.

INGREDIENTS

Dressing Bits
Juice of 1 lemon
¼ cup extra-virgin olive oil
½ teaspoon salt
½ teaspoon freshly ground white or black pepper
¼ teaspoon red chili flakes
1 small clove of garlic, chopped
Pinch of MSG (optional)

Vegetable Bits
≈4 cups well-cleaned, perfectly fresh *Portulaca oleracea* leaves
1 large shallot, peeled and very finely diced
1 red pepper,* finely diced

DIRECTIONS

First make the dressing by just shaking the dressing ingredients together in a jar. Now simply mix the leaves together with the dressing, shallots and diced red pepper in a bowl. Serve immediately!

Fun note: *Portulaca oleracea* is also interesting when pickled to make a relish. See Leda Meredith's *The Forager's Feast.*

*Not a fan of red peppers? Perhaps try using a firm but perfectly ripe Roma tomato, seeded.

"NO! THEY'RE ALL GONNA LAUGH AT YOU!"

Roasted Dandelion Flower Salad

Roasting fresh dandelion (*Taraxacum officinale*) flowers with a little good olive oil and tossing them in a dandelion greens salad is the optimal way to "weed" a garden! Dandelions are available all the time, but do always look for young, tender leaves. While even the most elderly guinea pigs will risk falling out of their cages to get at big dandelion leaves (and I have the videos to prove it), big leaves are bitter. Effortlessly make your dandelions produce nice tender leaves year-round by chopping them off at their bases regularly instead of foolishly pulling them out of the ground.

INGREDIENTS

Salad Bits
≈3 cups freshly picked whole dandelion flowers, clean and dry
Olive oil
Kosher salt
Few twists of freshly ground black pepper
≈2 cups tender dandelion* leaves, washed, dry and clean, and torn into bite-size pieces

Optional (adds nice color): ¼ cup finely chopped fresh red pepper†
Optional but tasty: a few sliced or diced hard-boiled eggs

Dressing Bits
1 pinch brown or white sugar
½ teaspoon kosher salt
¼ teaspoon white pepper
1 very finely minced shallot
1 very finely minced garlic clove
1 teaspoon Dijon mustard
1 tablespoon mayonnaise or sour cream
¼ cup top-notch extra-virgin olive oil
¼ cup red wine vinegar
½ teaspoon fresh thyme

DIRECTIONS

Set your broiler to high and the oven rack to the second to the top notch in your oven. In a medium-sized bowl, drizzle some olive oil over the flowers and gently stir with your hand to coat the flowers well. Sprinkle on some salt and freshly ground black pepper. Spread the flowers on a metal pan lined with foil or parchment paper to keep yourself from losing your mind over the cleanup process later. Pop in the oven. Set the timer for 3-4 minutes.

While your flowers are in the oven, work on the dressing. Put everything together in a small jar with a tight lid. Close lid and shake vigorously. Taste. Adjust seasonings as needed.

Check on the flowers. You may want to broil approximately another 1-2 minutes or until they are shrunken, soft and darkened. You want them crisp on the outside and the inner part cooked until soft. You do want to let them get sufficiently crisped (*id est* almost burned).

When the flowers are cooked to your satisfaction, bring them out of the oven to cool. Toss the dressing, torn dandelion leaves, and peppers together. Top with the roasted flowers. Arrange the hard-boiled eggs and red peppers around the scene as you prefer. Serve!

*Substitute chopped Tuscan kale or tender young red chard leaves if you are lazy. I have also used gai lan leaves, ribs removed. Yum!

†You may roast the chopped red peppers along with the flowers if you like. Put them on a separate piece of foil as the peppers will likely require more time in the oven than the flowers.

Seriously Thistle Salad

What is an artichoke but an overgrown (I mean "carefully bred for flavor and texture over millennia") thistle? This dish uses the tender parts of thistle plants, which taste a bit like artichokes or celery to me. The best time is when the flowers haven't opened yet, which is spring. You are mainly looking for chubby stems, and/but small, tender leaves are needed, too.

Always make sure you have correctly identified your thistle plants—you want milk thistle (purple flower, Latin name *Silybum marianum**) or sow thistle (yellow flower, Latin name *Sonchus oleraceus*).

Random tips! Harvesting thistles involves gloves, a knife and scissors, plus containers to hold the edible bits until you get home. While wearing gloves, grab the flower and strip all the leaves off the stem with a knife. Snip or chop the stem at the bottom of the plant. Peel the stem back in strips with a paring knife. Chop the inner part into bite sized pieces. The stems are ready to cook when the spines are completely gone.

For the leaves, be sure to cut all spines completely off with scissors.†

INGREDIENTS

≈2 cups thistle stems, peeled, chopped, washed and dried
¼ cup very finely chopped red onion or shallots
1 tablespoon chopped pickled nasturtium (*Tropaeolum*) seed pods
2 teaspoons white sugar (more to taste)
¼-½ teaspoon kosher salt
¼ teaspoon freshly ground black pepper
2-3 tablespoons red wine vinegar
2-3 tablespoons top-quality olive oil
1 cup tender thistle leaves, all spines removed, washed, dried, and well chopped or torn

DIRECTIONS

Steam the thistle stems until just barely fork tender, just a few
minutes in a basket steamer over boiling water. Allow to cool
completely.

Mix everything all together in a big bowl, starting with the dressing
items to be sure they blend together well. Stir in the plant material
with your hands, as this the proper way to stir and blend any salad.
Add more salt and pepper to taste! Serve immediately.

*Milk thistle is classified as a noxious weed in King County—few in
the know would complain about your tearing it up for food.

†Not so happy with the intensity of the spines on the thistle leaves
you find? Substitute another green of your preference such as turnip
greens, mustard, or kale! You may also substitute raw, peeled
broccoli stalks for the thistle stems, but in that case, there is no need
to bother steaming then, just cut into thin matchsticks.

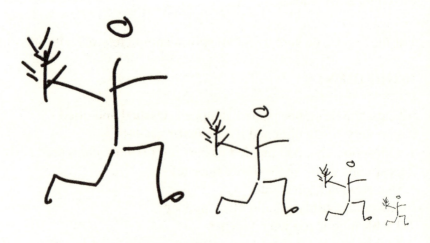

SAPIENS' QUEST FOR THISTLE

Spring Flower Salad

Warning! Fancy pants alert! Enlist some knowledgeable friends to find all the various tidbits in this salad. Everything goes more quickly when multiple people can spread out across a garden or any other weedy area where you have permission to harvest. I recommend having the dressing on hand before you go foraging so you can throw everything together as soon as you get to a kitchen. As the title implies, this recipe should be pulled off in spring when all these greens are small and tender. Note that where I say, "petals only," I mean just gently pull the petals off the flower base.

SALAD INGREDIENTS

Dressing Bits
1 generous pinch brown or white sugar
1 teaspoon kosher salt
½ teaspoon white pepper
3 tablespoons very finely minced shallots
1 very finely minced clove of garlic
1 tablespoon Dijon mustard
½ cup top-notch extra virgin olive oil
¼-½ cup red wine vinegar
½-1 teaspoon dried herb of your choice (optional, there's already a lot going on)

Salad Bits
1 cup miner's lettuce (*Claytonia perfoliata*)
1 cup sheep sorrel (*Rumex acetosella*)
½ cups tender plantago (*Plantago lanceolata* or *Plantago major*) leaves
½ cup tender red amaranth (*Amaranthus cruentus*) leaves
1 cup tender dandelion (*Taraxacum officinale*) leaves, torn
15-20 young plantago (*Plantago lanceolata* or *Plantago major*) flower stalks,* steamed until just al dente
1-2 peeled and chopped young thistle (*Silybum marianum* or *Sonchus oleraceus*) stems

5-10 red clover (*Trifolium pratense*) flowers, petals only

2-3 dandelion flowers, petals only
4-5 chicory (*Cichorium intybus*) flowers, petals only

5-10 whole fireweed (*Chamaenerion angustifolium*)† flowers, fully intact
8-10 whole violet (*Viola spp.*, any common variety) flowers, yellow or purple, fully intact
4-6 whole daisy (*Bellis perennis*) flowers, fully intact

DIRECTIONS

First make the dressing. Put everything together in a small jar with a tight lid. Close lid and shake vigorously. Taste. Adjust seasonings (salt, sugar, pepper) as you feel necessary.

Put all the plant bits except the flowers in a large bowl and toss very gently with your hands to combine. Add the dressing, using an amount of your preference, and toss again gently. Distribute into bowls for serving and top artistically with the flower petals and whole flowers. Serve immediately to keep the artistic gestalt intact!

*Pro tip: this is the part of the plantain that looks vaguely like skinny, bumpy asparagus stalks, before the flowers form.

†I will not talk about *Chamaenerion angustifolium* elsewhere but here's a tidbit of information about this beautiful plant. The innards of the young stalks are sweet, and you can try scraping them out with your teeth (as you would scrape artichoke bracts) for a small treat. We have a few different kinds of fireweed in the Seattle area. If you find them growing in an area where you can pick them legally, play with a few stems and see what you think!

SAVORY WARM DISHES

While I have always had a penchant for sweets, it seems that as I continue to subject my novelty-seeking palate to new flavors, I am continually more enamored with savory foods. I am therefore especially excited to share this selection of savory discoveries with my readers. As I mentioned in the introduction, a key objective of this book, and particularly with this section, is to firmly do away with notions of foraged foods being bland survival foods, reserved for gulping down uncomfortably under a leaky tarp in the woods. The following dishes are meant to be cooked in the warm, dry, and cozy comfort of home (or any friendly kitchen, really).

Each dish presented here should be part of a meal. That is, each dish should ideally be served alongside something else, such as a protein, carbohydrate, or salad— whatever seems good. While I trust you to use your own vividly creative imagination when pairing dishes, I have attempted to make a few random suggestions with each recipe.

In this section, I am especially jazzed to share the Persian recipes with you—these are the quince stew and fig leaf non-dolmeh pilaf casserole. I have cross checked the recipes and ingredients with my friends in Iran and got the thumbs up (wink if you know what thumbs up means in Iran). Hey, did the mention of cooking with fig leaves pique your interest? Many people are unaware that fig leaves are edible at all! Tender fig leaves are plentiful in spring and have a nutty taste. If you like, you can prepare dolmeh with them. It can be fun to make a large amount of dolmeh with friends, so consider inviting hungry creative types over to prepare and eat said dolmeh together if you are inspired. But my similarly tasty recipe in this section is what I call the distracted cook's version. When in doubt, or in a hurry, let's KISS—Keep It Simple, Stupid!

Italian Chicory Sauté

Chicory is known for its root, which is tasty coffee substitute, or as a coffee blend, which is a regional specialty of New Orleans. But *this* dish takes a stab at the hearty leaves and stems! The recipe is based on a traditional Italian recipe I came across while reading compilations of old regional recipes during some travels in Italy.

Identify your chicory plants (*Cichorium intybus*) in the autumn so when they come up again in spring, you will recognize the plants early, before they get tough and bitter. Wild chicory greens are already strongly-flavored in spring and turn increasingly tough and bitter as summer progresses. Chopped chard makes a good substitute but the boiling time for chard will be minimal. Cultivated chicory is also a good substitute when you can find it.

INGREDIENTS

500 grams (≈2 cups) tender, small chicory stems and leaves
2 tablespoons olive oil
1-2 cloves of garlic, chopped
1 small red onion, finely chopped
½ teaspoon kosher salt (plus more to taste)
1 cup cooked cannellini beans (optional but good)
hot pepper flakes, to taste
fresh thyme leaves, to taste

DIRECTIONS

Cut chicory stems into tiny pieces, then cook in a small amount of boiling water just until tender. Take out with a slotted spoon and drain well. Next put the chicory leaves into the boiling water. Cook until just tender. This time will vary depending on the starting point of the tenderness/toughness of the chicory. Spoon out leaves and drain well, then chop toughly on a cutting board. Pour the leftover bitter pot water into your garden!

In an appropriately sized frying pan, fry the red onion and garlic in the olive oil until translucent, then add the cooked chicory, salt and hot pepper flakes to taste. Stir/toss the beans and thyme in gently, and heat just into combined (just a couple minutes should do it). Consume!

But Wait! Here Is A Gut-Busting Option!

To make this a heavier, heartier dish, fry up some of the best chopped bacon you can find (using from 150 to no more than 300 grams), then fry the chicory in the bacon grease instead of the olive oil. Bam! Finally stir the cooked greens together with about 300 grams of perfectly al dente tagliatelle pasta. Pass some parmesan cheese for extra heft. Loosen your belt discreetly post-meal.

TEAM INTYBUS

Tangy Middle Eastern Style Mallow*

Make a fun greens side dish with all that dwarf mallow (*Malva neglecta*) or common mallow (*Malva sylvestris*) that you discover in your derelict yard or community garden. I have learned that mallows are a popular vegetable in Turkey and there the big leaves area fried into chips, used to wrap dolmeh, or made into tea. Double this recipe, and serve with long grain rice and a protein, if you want something more substantial. Three cups of fresh leaves will cook down to practically nothing! I see a lot of good-looking mallow around in October through December. Substitute tender kale or spinach greens if mallows elude you.

INGREDIENTS

2 tablespoons olive oil
≈3 cups *Malva neglecta* and/or *Malva sylvestris* leaves, thoroughly washed and well chopped
All the skinny stems of the mallow leaves, chopped very finely
Pinch of kosher salt
Pinch of freshly ground black pepper
1 small onion, diced
1 garlic clove, chopped (optional)
½ lemon, ready to squeeze with impunity

Optional but elevating:
Extra-virgin olive oil
Dried sumac
A few dried barberries, chopped small
Lemon wedges

DIRECTIONS

Heat a good non-stick skillet to medium heat. Add olive oil and the onion. Sauté around a few minutes or more, until the onions look like you probably could eat them. Now add the mallow stems. Sauté a moment to soften. Now add the leaves. Sauté further. Salt and pepper go in next. Squeeze in the lemon juice, stir, and it should look good and be ready to plate. So, plate it and serve.

If you would like to make this look fancy post-plating, top with a splash of olive oil, a sprinkle of sumac and a few dried barberries for visual contrast. Add a wedge of lemon to the food landscape for additional sexiness.

Mallow is naturally a tiny bit slimy, so do eat this while it is hot. Leftovers may have a curious texture, but I think this vegetable is delicious and the texture is negligible.

Note: If the leaves are big enough, as they could be with *Malva sylvestris,* the leaves make excellent dolmeh! See *The Forager's Feast* by Lera Meredith.

*Another tasty plant to consider in this dish could be bindweed (Hedge bindweed is *Calystegia sepium* and field bindweed is *Convolvulus arvensis*). I received this suggestion from Arthur Lee Jacobson, who asserts that cooked bindweed is tasty and plentiful.

AWKWARD MALLOW FAMILY PHOTO

Easy Spicy Field Mustard

This dish packs a spicy punch! Be sure to correctly identify and use field mustard specifically because the larger category *Brassica rapa* includes several other popular vegetables, including turnips, bok choy, and cime di rapa. Confused about ID? Arthur Lee Jacobson carefully describes and extols the tasty virtues of *Brassica rapa var. campestris* in his book *Wild Plants of Greater Seattle*.

INGREDIENTS

2 tablespoons oil
≈3 cups field mustard,* leaves and stems, leaves torn, any stems cut very small (as small as you can bear)
3 cloves garlic, chopped
2 red Thai mouse turd chilies, cut lengthways
¼ cup chicken or vegetable broth
Kosher salt to taste
Red pepper flakes to taste
Few pinches of palm or brown sugar

DIRECTIONS

Have all your ingredients ready because this will go quickly. Heat up a wok or large frying pan to high heat. Throw in the oil and garlic, stir, then add the field mustard and the mouse turd chili. Stir quickly. The mustard will start to wilt. Throw in the broth, stir, and cover. Have a peek after about 1 minute. Beware the spicy fumes from the chili. Does it need a dab of water to keep cooking without scorching? Maybe add a few drops. Toss in some salt in to taste. How's the broth situation? Keep tossing things around in the pan.

When it looks like it is getting pretty close to something you want to eat, sprinkle on some sugar and a dash of red pepper flakes, stir well to distribute and turn onto a cool plate. Serve with rice (of course) and a nice protein.† If you are a spice maniac, you may also want to have vinegar-pickled chilies on the table as a condiment.

*You guessed it, standard cultivated mustard greens from your garden, the farmer's market, Asian grocery or any well-stocked grocery store will do!

†Speaking of protein, I recommend this with some firm (but not extra firm), pan-fried seasoned tofu. But many people love it with pork (similar to southern fried greens with ham hock). It is up to you!

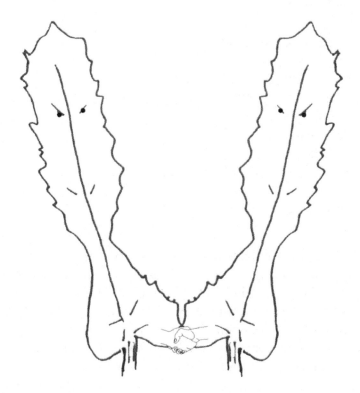

MUSTARD PACT

Sautéed Daylilies

I discovered this dish while living in Thailand. There is some debate about whether or not daylily (*Hemerocallis fulva*) is fully edible, but I do not recall any adverse effects from eating it occasionally in Thailand, and historically it has been eaten around the world without (commonly known) negative impact to humans. The buds are naturally peppery tasting, but you can add a Thai mouse turd chili or red pepper flakes to the dish if you want to make it significantly spicier. The plants generate buds almost all summer, allowing multiple opportunities to try this dish

INGREDIENTS

3-4 tablespoons canola oil
2-3 cups daylily buds
2-4 cloves garlic, chopped
2-3 tablespoons vegetable broth
Kosher salt to taste
Pinch of sugar
Pinch of MSG
Freshly ground white pepper, to taste

DIRECTIONS

Have all your ingredients ready because this will go quickly. Heat up a wok or large frying pan to high heat. Throw in the oil and garlic, stir, then add the daylily buds. Stir quickly. Throw in the broth, stir, and cover. Have a peek after about 1 minute. Does it need a dab of broth to keep cooking without scorching? If yes, splash in and stir. Note that you do want these crisp and hot, not soft and floppy, so it's better to under cook than to overcook. When they look cheerfully bright, close to something you want to eat, sprinkle on the salt, sugar and MSG, then turn them out onto a cool serving plate. Top generously with the freshly ground white pepper. Serve with rice and a nice protein.

Very Creamy "Any Greens" Soup

Use any foraged green for this soup! This is based on classic style cream soup. Be sure to use a green, or a mix of greens, that you enjoy because the soup will taste like that green! Fun options are stinging nettle (*Urtica dioica*), watercress (*Nasturtium officinale*), dandelion (*Taraxacum officinale*), field mustard (*Brassica rapa var. campestris* and even clovers (*Trifolium repens* and *Trifolium pratense*). Use already cooked potatoes if you have them on hand and hanker to use leftovers.

INGREDIENTS

ICH BIN

SUPPE

1-2 cloves chopped garlic
1 large chopped shallot
2-3 tablespoons unsalted butter

4 packed cups any chopped foraged greens
4 cups veg or chicken broth of your choice
1 chopped Russet potato (≈250 grams)
2 chopped gold potatoes (≈250 grams)
¼-½ teaspoon black or white pepper
½-1 teaspoon salt
¼-½ cup heavy cream or Greek yogurt or a combination (optional)

DIRECTIONS

Sweat the garlic and shallots in the butter on medium heat. When everything looks translucent, add the greens and let them wilt a bit. Add the broth, potatoes, salt, and pepper. Bring to a boil and then cook on medium heat, stirring occasionally until the potatoes are sufficiently soft—perhaps 20 minutes. Add a little more broth if needed as you go along. When the potatoes are soft, take off the heat, cool, then puree everything in small batches in a good blender. Add some heavy cream, more broth, or a touch of water now if it seems too thick. Serve with a little swirl of cream or yogurt, a nice crusty bread and maybe a beet salad for fun color contrasts!

Grilled Cheese Chickweed Hummus Sandwich

Chickweed, *Stellaria media*, is much better in sandwiches than plain lettuce or bean sprouts— plus, it is free, guaranteed fresh, and you do not have to hassle much to prepare them. Chickweed is most prolific almost any time of the year besides the heat of summer, but I like to collect them around early December. When you harvest, do be sure you are getting the chickweed and not the other plants (such as grass) that tend to grow mixed in with chickweed. This recipe is for one sandwich and you can figure it out from here if you want more.

INGREDIENTS

Very big handful of fresh and clean chickweed, well chopped
1 teaspoon olive oil
½ teaspoon vinegar
Sprinkle of salt and pepper

1-2 tablespoons mayonnaise
1-2 teaspoon chili paste, such as sambal oelek or Lao chili oil

¼ cup hummus*
1 big, thin slice of a very sweet, crispy white onion
1 slice of Swiss or provolone cheese
Couple slices rye bread or whatever tasty and firm bread floats your boat at the moment

Olive oil for your frying pan

DIRECTIONS

Stir together the chickweed with oil, vinegar, salt and pepper.

Mix the chili paste and mayonnaise together, then spread on the bread. Spread hummus on bread. Add cheese. Grease a frying pan well and fry the sandwich on both sides over medium heat until yummy. Consider pressing the sandwich with a weight (I use a teapot filled with water with a piece of foil under it) while you fry it if you are interested in a "Cuban press" type situation. Pressing the sandwich pretty much guarantees it will not fall apart when flipping, as well.

After it is fried to your tastes, open up the sandwich on the hummus-bread side and stuff the dressed chickweed and the onion slices into the sandwich. This creates a nice crispy hot-cold contrast that you hopefully find entertaining. This sandwich is also delicious paired with pickled green tomatoes if you have luckily acquired some!

*Not a hummus fan? Try a veggie burger, a split pea burger, an actual burger, a fried marinated tofu slab, a slab of tempeh, some roasted mushrooms or whatever other savory thing seems like it would be a good idea in such a sandwich.

TRICKY CHICKWEED

Baked Chickweed-Flickweed Gnudi

Why not put the wild greens flavors of some *Stellaria media* and *Cardamine hirsuta* into some savory Italian gnudi? Chickweed (*Stellaria media*) is very mild-mannered but flickweed (*Cardamine hirsuta,* also called bittercress) gets this name because when it goes to seed, the seeds will shoot everywhere. I pick both plants in December, well before the flickweed gets tough and seed-ridden. This recipe only requires one fluffy handful of a half-half mix of the greens. Double that if you are bold!

This makes a modest amount, but it is easy to double the recipe. Note that gnudi are usually boiled and then baked, but I found that straight up baking them is delicious, so let us skip the risky boiling and see how many Italians I can tick off with such sacrilege.

INGREDIENTS

1-2 tablespoons butter

400 grams whole milk ricotta cheese, ideally drained overnight in a strainer lined with a cheesecloth
20 grams finely chopped sautéed and cooled *Stellaria media* and *Cardamine hirsuta** (about a handful fresh)
2 tablespoons well-crushed breadcrumbs (brioche is yum)
¼ cup shredded parmesan cheese
20 grams all-purpose flour
½ teaspoon kosher salt
⅛ teaspoon freshly ground black pepper
Few bold strokes of freshly grated nutmeg
1 egg yolk

More parmesan cheese
More breadcrumbs
Your favorite savory mushroom pasta sauce (perhaps a porcini sauce, since porcini grow in our area, but I have only made cremini)
A big handful of chopped fresh Italian herbs (I use flat leaf parsley)

DIRECTIONS

Melt butter is a small casserole dish (I use a small 8.5 x 6.5 or a slightly larger 7.5 x 11.5 glass dish). Heat oven to 350° F.

Mix the ricotta, cooked and chopped greens, cheese, flour, breadcrumbs, salt, pepper, nutmeg and eggs together. Form into ¾ inch balls and put in the buttered dish.

Top the gnudi generously with more breadcrumbs and parmesan cheese. Bake for 30-40 minutes or until they look like something delicious. Top with the prepared sauce of your choice and throw on the fresh herbs. You can keep it just warm at 200° F at this point if you want for another 30ish minutes. I serve a small amount of gnudi with a big fresh salad because the gnudi are so delightfully rich.

*Not into these greens or having trouble locating them? Combine with (or replace with) well chopped different cooked greens, like mallow (*Malva neglecta or Malva sylvestris*), lamb's quarters (*Chenopodium album*), watercress (*Nasturtium officinale*), stinging nettles (*Urtica dioica*), arugula, or even regular ol' spinach (gasp!).

Sri Lankan Style Greens

How I got so interested in Sri Lanka way back in high school is a convoluted story, but basically it started because the country name appeared on a list of possible places to find a pen-pal and I thought, "cool country name." Seven years later, I was in Sri Lanka cooking dinner with my pen-pal's mom! Yes, it is true you will not find fresh coconuts growing locally in Seattle, but, hey, I never promised you a coconut garden.

INGREDIENTS

1 large shallot, chopped small
2 tablespoons coconut oil
1 tablespoon whole black mustard seeds
≈3-4 cups, packed well-chopped tender foraged greens
¼ cup fresh shredded coconut
1 teaspoon kosher salt (more to taste)
1-inch piece fresh turmeric root, finely grated
1 red Thai mouse turd chili, whole, stem intact if possible

Lime or lemon juice to taste (half a fruit? You decide)

DIRECTIONS

In a big frying pan, sauté the shallot in the oil until translucent. Add the mustard seeds, red chili, and turmeric. Crank up to high heat. Be prepared to put the chopped greens into the pan as soon as the mustard seeds want to start popping out. Stir!

Right after the greens, add the coconut and salt. Stir! Splash a tad of water or more coconut oil into the pan if needed to cook things along. You want this dish dry-fried and crumbly-feeling.

Sauté for 2-3 minutes or until all looks tasty, then transfer to a plate and spritz all with lemon or lime juice. Serve! Best with Sri Lankan string hoppers, appam and lentil soup. Dunno? Look them up—yum!

Persian Quince Stew

Quince (*Cydonia oblonga*) is exciting in Persian recipes. This is sweet, tangy, and savory stew that I tasted while in Iran. The recipe makes quite a bit, so make a half recipe if you are not sure you will like it. With good long grain rice and fresh herbs as a garnish, I think it is fantastic, although it is not particularly attractive looking. In this dish, use fist-sized quince and make sure they are well-peeled, since the thick peels can be distractingly rough. If you feel the flavor is bland at the end of cooking, it is perfectly OK to add salt (or, *gasp*, MSG!) to taste.

The majority of quince are not edible straight off the tree, and Seattle folks who have inherited a tree sometimes do not know what they are. You will see the quinces ripening in October and November, sometimes later. Quince are *very* easy to procure from people who are disinclined to cooking them! When they smell fragrant and start to fall off the tree, they are definitely ripe.

INGREDIENTS

1 large white onion, chopped into bite-sized chunks
2-3 tablespoons mild olive oil
450 grams (≈1 pound) chopped chicken, any parts considered edible (vegans, please replace with seitan*)
2 teaspoons salt
1 teaspoon freshly ground black pepper
3 cups water
3 quinces,† cored and peeled
Juice of 2 limes
½ cup dried apricots or prunes or a combination, chopped into small pieces
4-5 firm yellow potato, cut in chunks

Somewhat optional but awesome and highly recommended Persian style side dish garnishes: handfuls of flat-leaf parsley, mint, basil, cilantro, dill, tarragon, chives, marjoram and sliced radishes. Or, if you are lazy, handfuls of arugula are passable.

DIRECTIONS

In a big saucepan or low-slung soup pot, sweat the onion in olive oil until the onion looks translucent. Add the meat; cover and cook until meat is cooked, stirring occasionally. Add salt and pepper.

Add water, lime juice, quince, apricots/prunes, and potatoes. Simmer, covered, for 1 hour,†† stirring occasionally until meat is tender.

Serve with freshly steamed long grain rice and eat sprigs of fresh (trimmed and washed/dried only) herbs and radish slices as you go along.

*Yes, old school seitan. But you can try other more new-fangled things. This dish needs to include a very savory but mild tasting element to balance the sweet and sour of the various fruits.

†Substitute up to one firm apple if you only have a couple quince, but do not entirely replace the quince! This dish is about the quince!

††This is a great slower cooker recipe. If you are into it, try this recipe in the slow cooker from the simmering point onward.

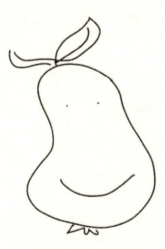

QUINCE CHARMING

Fig Leaf Non-Dolmeh Pilaf Casserole

Not just for covering the adorable privates of marble statues anymore, tender fig leaves from the *Ficus carica* tree can be like grape leaves for dolmeh (or dolma if you are thinking of the Greek option). However, as the recipe title suggests, I won't go into that here because making dolmeh is, let's say, effortful. Fig leaves have a nutty, sweet flavor. Choose young leaves in spring that are about the size of your hand. To pick the leaves, just snip them off the tree at the very base of the stem. If you do goof up with your leaf selection and you find that they are too fibrous to consume even after cooking, know that you can still eat the casserole innards.

This is a well-herbed recipe! You can add even more herbs if you want. Feel free to also add dried barberries, preserved lemon, and ground sumac, to your taste. My son likes this slightly dry dish best when paired with roasted eggplant in garlicy tomato sauce.

INGREDIENTS

1 cup long grain basmati rice
Olive oil
2 cups finely diced white onion
1 clove finely diced garlic
230 grams (≈ ½ pound) ground beef*
3 cups fresh flat leaf parsley, chopped small, including stems
1 teaspoon dried tarragon
1 tablespoon tomato paste diluted in 1 tablespoon water
1 teaspoon kosher salt
½ teaspoon freshly ground black pepper
30-40 tender fig leaves
Zest of one lemon
Juice of one lemon mixed with ¼ cup water and ¼ teaspoon salt

DIRECTIONS

Steam rice in a rice cooker first. You want it cool when you add to the rest of the filling. While that's happening, sauté the onions and garlic until cooked through, then add meat and cook further. Add herbs and salt. Add tomato paste. Take off the stove and allow to cool completely. Gently add the cooled cooked rice and lemon zest. Taste. It may need much more salt and pepper.

Now it is probably time to prepare the leaves. In a small amount of just barely boiling water, cook the leaves until they are tender enough to bite through. The time will vary, so be sure to test a few and see how long it takes for an average-sized leaf to be biteable. Use tongs or a slotted spoon to assist your travails.

Spread some olive oil at the bottom of a ceramic or glass dish. I usually use an 11x7 dish for a taller casserole, but you can go with a larger casserole for a thinner finished product. Cover the bottom of the dish completely with one or two or more layers of the cooked leaves.

Dump the rice-meat-herbs mixture on top of the leaves and smooth it out. Now cover all of the rice with two or more layers of fig leaves.

Cover tightly with foil and bake at 350° for 60 solid minutes. At 60 minutes, pour the salted water-and-lemon juice on the top of the leaves. Bake another 30 minutes.

Serve hot or at room temperature with delicious juicy things, such as gigante beans, roasted eggplant and tomato as I mentioned above, and perhaps Persian *maast-o-khiar* (a yogurt dressing, similar to Indian raita) as a condiment.

*If you want to avoid beef, consider different savory foodstuffs, such as a mixture of cooked cubed yellow potato, pine nuts and additional onions and herbs—these will need more salt and perhaps a wee tad more tomato paste to boost the umami.

Sesame Burdock Root

Burdock (*Arctium minus*) is plentiful in Seattle. The high-fiber low-calorie root, in its first year of growth, can be harvested year-round as long as you can identify the plant accurately. However, I have read that autumn is the best harvest time. Second year plants are tall and known for their burs, the inspiration for Velcro, but the roots will be spent. This recipe is a Korean way to prepare burdock, so, I like it with white rice, bulgogi, and a bite of kimchi on the side.

INGREDIENTS

250 grams (≈1½ - 2 cups) burdock root,* washed and peeled
1 tablespoon sesame oil
1 tablespoon canola oil

1½-2 tablespoons soy sauce
1 tablespoon neutral tasting honey
¼-⅓ cup water

Sesame seeds
Red pepper flakes

DIRECTIONS

First peel and carefully cut the root to make matchstick-type shavings. Look for a video online called *Sasagaki Gobo - How to cut gobo (burdock root)* by Japanese superfood cooking to witness an excellent quality burdock cutting technique.

Heat a large non-stick frying pan to medium-high heat. Add the burdock root and the oils. Stir-fry until translucent. This takes a little time and depends on the size of your frying pan. You may add a splash of water here and there to help steam it along.

Pour in the soy sauce, water, and honey or sugar. Stir well then simmer over medium heat until the liquid has evaporated, about 7 to 8 minutes. Sprinkle with as much sesame seeds and red pepper flakes as you like, and taste. You will notice that the burdock is still pleasantly crunchy. It might want another splash of soy sauce. Still bland? Sprinkle on a pinch of sugar and a tad of MSG if you have it! Now turn onto a plate and serve. It is also tasty room temperature or cold, so do not sweat it if you have other things to do first.

*You can substitute firm white sweet potato for the burdock but please understand that it will cook faster and turn out sweeter than the burdock, so you will want to adjust the honey/sugar situation and the cooking time, too.

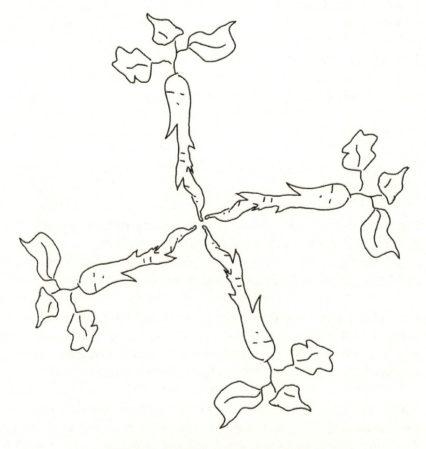

SYNCHRONIZED BURDOCK SWIMMERS

UNAPOLOGETIC DESSERTS

As I mentioned in the Sweet Snacks section, who can resist sweets? I mean, *I* can, occasionally, and I bet *you* can too, but look, I am sure we know *someone* who struggles like a fly caught in a sugary web, right? So, this section is for them. Or perhaps rather for *you*, as you deviously worm your way into the sweets lover's heart.

Following we have a few baked items, a jam and two candies with suggestions. I think the items included here are extremely tasty but that is nothing terribly surprising when it comes to disaccharides! You could consider starting in this section if you would like to convince your sweets-loving sweeties to go on some foraging expeditions with you. Some heretofore reluctant kids may become oddly enthusiastic about berry picking if they know the literal fruits of their effort will be going into the jam on their morning toast. If all else fails, I believe that these items, especially the candies, make uniquely impressive seasonal gifts.

While I feel like a bit of a slacker for only including about seven recipes here, you will see there are a variety of suggestions for taking some of these items further, in different directions, if you like. See how I have thoughtfully provided you with creative freedom, rather than excessively dogmatic complexity?

Huckle-Salal-Blackberry Cobbler

Summer goodness. These fruits will all be ripe at the same time. I say this dessert will help you work your way toward a deeper appreciation of salal (*Gaultheria shallon*), especially when secretly paired with the sexier red huckleberries (*Vaccinium parvifolium*), or just plain old blueberries, *plus* blackberries (*Rubus armeniacus)* in a dessert. You won't know what hit ya!

INGREDIENTS

Fruit filling
2-3 tablespoons butter (for buttering the baking dish)
200 grams brown sugar
35 grams tapioca starch
¼ teaspoon kosher salt
Few bold gratings of freshly ground nutmeg
250 grams huckleberries (or blueberries)
250 grams salal (*Gaultheria shallon*) berries
500 grams fresh blackberries

Topping
65 grams all-purpose flour
100 grams white whole wheat flour
2 tablespoons turbinado sugar
1½ teaspoons baking powder
½ teaspoon kosher salt
100 grams (7 tablespoons) cold butter, cut into ¼-inch cubes
⅓ cup cold buttermilk
More turbinado sugar for sprinkling on top

DIRECTIONS

Butter up a 7- by 11-inch glass baking dish. Preheat oven to 400° F. In a large bowl, whisk together sugar, tapioca starch, salt, nutmeg, and baking soda until well combined. Add berries and stir quite gently to get them evenly coated. Put into baking dish.

Now make the topping. In a mixing bowl, stir together the flours, flour, sugar, baking powder, and salt. Add butter and cut in with a pastry cutter or two knives until pea-sized. Stir in milk or buttermilk with a clunky spoon until just *barely* combined. Drop dough in small tablespoon-sized spoonfuls, evenly dispersed, over the fruit. Sprinkle top with a little more turbinado sugar, if you like, for a crunchy texture.

Bake in that 400° F oven until the topping is rich golden brown, typically about 60 minutes. You may need to tent foil over it starting at 45 minutes to keep the browning in check. Cool at least an hour before serving.

No brainer suggestion: great with ice cream and/or whipped cream!

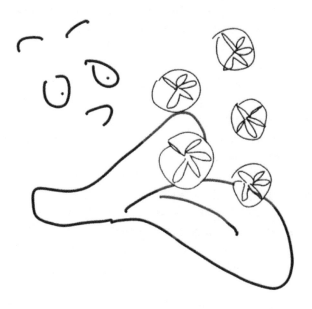

GOTTA CATCH EM ALL: SALAL

Desert King Fig Tart

Ficus carica is a great tree with many interesting varieties of fruit in addition to its edible leaves (see Fig Leaf Non-Dolmeh Pilaf Casserole). A pretty variety of fig called Desert King is usually ready to pick around July. Yes, that name is Desert King, like the king of a desert, not the king of desserts (although maybe it could be). If you haven't already eaten all the Desert King figs you find fresh, why not try making this pretentious tart? Dessert king figs are ready when you grab them on the tree and they are soft, but not so soft that they have already split open. Note that these figs are always green, even when ripe, and their innards are pink and suggestive.

There are some other varieties of figs in Seattle that ripen later, but Desert King is my favorite. So, if you miss the harvest in July, there's certainly no harm in testing the other fig varieties in autumn!

If this crust sounds a little complex, I recommend going with the perfect pate brisee recipe in Jacquy Pfeiffer's awesome book, *The Art of French Pastry*. You will Lose. Your. Mind.

INGREDIENTS

Crust
140 grams pastry flour
⅛ teaspoon kosher salt
⅛ teaspoon baking powder

90 grams cold unsalted butter,* cut in small cubes
60 grams cold mascarpone cheese, cut† in small cubes
Finely grated rind of one small lemon

¼ cup very cold brandy or other liquor of your choice

A little powdered sugar for dusting the crust when rolling

Filling

12-14 large fresh and very ripe Desert King figs, quartered
2-3 tablespoons brandy or other liquor of your choice
¼ cup turbinado sugar
¼ teaspoon kosher salt
2-3 tablespoons cold butter, cut into ¼ inch cubes††

Optional: apricot jam

DIRECTIONS

For the crust, put the dry things in a large bowl. Using a pastry
cutter, cut in the butter and cheese until dough looks like large peas.
At the midpoint of cutting, add the lemon zest and incorporate well.
Sprinkle on the salt. Sprinkle on the cold alcohol. Push together
dough with your hands until you have made a ball. It should go
together well but still be just a wee tab crumbly, and you do not want
it to be entirely uniform looking—you want to see chunks of butter
and cheese in it. Push it together tightly and form into a disk. Wrap
tightly in plastic wrap and refrigerate a few hours or overnight.

When you think you are about ready to bake, bring your crust dough
ever so slightly closer to room temperature while you prepare the
filling by very gently stirring the filling items together in a medium
sized bowl. Set aside.

Preheat oven to 400° F. Grab a 9½ inch tart pan with a removable
bottom.

Roll out the dough very gradually and slowly between two pieces of
wax paper that you have dusted with powdered sugar. You want the
dough to be as thin as possible (¼ inch is too thick). If it seems to get
too soft and sticky as you are rolling, which is likely, take it easy and
pop the dough back in the fridge about 5-10 minutes to firm up.
When the dough is rolled out enough that it extends well beyond the
tart pan edge, carefully peel off one side of the paper, position the

dough into the tart pan, and gently press the dough into the pan, carefully pulling away the paper as you go. Leave the dough well pushed against and hanging over the fluted edge of the pan. A standard tart making protocol is to leave the dough hanging over the edge of the pan, so you can trim the crust off evenly for a perfect edge with a sharp knife after it has baked. Of course, if that bothers you (as it does me), trim the dough as best you can to make it look tidy now, and use the bonus dough, cut in pieces and sprinkled with granulated sugar, to bake into crusty cookies.

Prick the bottom of the tart crust very well with a fork and then fill the crust with pie weights. Bake 15 minutes. Remove the weights. Boldly trim off the edges of the crust along the top with a very sharp knife if you left the dough hanging over the edge.

Stir the filling, put inside the tart crust and arrange the quartered figs so the whole thing looks pretty good, not too messy, or just as fancy as you want. Bake about 30 minutes or until the figs appear cooked and the crust is golden brown. Be sure to tent some aluminum foil over the pan while it cooks to control the browning of exposed crust.

Cool as well as you can bear. Carefully slide out of the tart pan onto an appropriate serving plate. If you want it to look glossy, mix a little apricot jam with water and brush on the fruit before serving. Top with real whipped cream and/or vanilla ice cream!

*Choose a low-water percentage/high fat percentage butter if you would like to avoid the tart crust shrinking. Otherwise, just expect it to shrink quite a bit— the more water in your butter, the more it will shrink when baked.

†It is not actually possible to cut mascarpone into cubes—spoon little dabs on a plate and stick it in the freezer for 10-15 minutes to form small firm blobs that you can cut into the flour.

††Are you perhaps a fan of ricotta cheese as well as (more) mascarpone cheese? Spoon teaspoon-size spoonfuls of either/both of these cheeses onto the tart after you have put the figs and butter

cubes into the tart crust. I think figs + ricotta is a *wow* flavor combination.

Secret, simple bonus fig pastry idea: I am not inclined to write another full recipe. Consider using some store-bought puff pastry to loosely wrap fig quarters, with a little scoop of the mascarpone cheese (or a different, perhaps savory, cheese?) plopped on their middles, a generous pinch of sugar, a pinch of chopped fennel flowers, dash of salt, and then bake in mini muffin tins at 425° F until schmexy* (15-20ish minutes is my best guess).

*"schmexy" = baked through.

More ridiculous thoughts: Baking maniacs may note that it is easy to apply the fig tart concept to other local fruits. You have my explicit permission to chop up a bunch of foraged fruits into similarly sized bits and just see how it goes — how about some huckleberry, fig and salal together? Or maybe just strawberries and figs? For pie-newbs, know that when you make additions and substitutions, remember to add a little cornstarch, tapioca, arrowroot or all-purpose flour with your filling for fruits that are low-pectin and tend to turn runny (notable low-pectin tricksters include blueberries, cherries, and strawberries).

FRUGAVORES IN LOVE

Strawberry Tree* Jam

Arbutus unedo, or strawberry tree, is a fun, very bumpy, gritty-textured fruit that is relatively popular in southern Europe, but it is almost entirely wasted in Seattle. Once you recognize this tree, you will see copious amounts of the fruit rotting on sidewalks in October and November.

This is a basic recipe. Double it if you want. There will probably be enough fruit around to make as much as you like. The fruits contain many bulky seeds and a lot of peels, so do not be terribly surprised by a modest final volume at the end of your cooking. There is plenty of pectin in the fruit, so do not wonder you need to add pectin or other pectin-containing fruit to firm it up. For me, 1 kilo of fruit tends to produce two cups of jam, so I prepare two 8-ounce jelly jars.

INGREDIENTS

At least 1 kilo completely fresh and ripe *Arbutus unedo* fruits, well washed
¾ cup sugar for every 1 cup of fruit pulp
1 small orange, lemon, or lime, juiced and zested, for every intended cup of fruit pulp

DIRECTIONS

Boil up your glass jars for containing your jam.

Put the fruits in an appropriately sized saucepan and heat up to get the fruit to disintegrate. Stir well as you go along, and it will soften and fall apart. It shouldn't take long.

Now smash the cooked fruit through a sieve. You can start with the food mill and then use the sieve, but you will need to use the sieve in the end to get all the detractors out, so I tend to skip the food mill. The seeds and skins will really be in your way— do your best— keep stirring and pressing and it will work.

Rinse out the saucepan so there aren't any gritty peels or seeds left in it! Measure your final amount of sieved fruit pulp, then add appropriate amount of sugar, orange, lemon or lime juice (plus the zest) in your saucepan. Boil, then stir and continue to stir with a wooden spoon for about 10-15 minutes until it coats the back of a spoon very well, or when you put it on a cold plate, it holds together and feels gel-like (or, if you are into thermometers, they say this is when you reach 220° F). Remove from the heat and pour into the boiled glass jars, then top with boiled lids.

Aside from boiling my jars, I make this in small quantities as a freezer jam and do not bother with proper canning, but you can totally do that if you know how. In my experience, this jam keeps for about six months in the freezer and a month or so in the fridge.

Serve with a nice tangy hard cheese such as parmesan or manchego. Or perhaps go soft and try it with some brie on wheat crackers. I put it on whole wheat brioche with mascarpone cheese, which is essentially mind-blowing. Or try it on or in whatever else you like (jam thumbprint cookies? Yum!). Even after sieving, it does maintain a slightly gritty texture, similar to fig or pear jam, so rest assured that you didn't make any mistakes if you still perceive a bit of pear-like texture when eating.

*Try a different fruit application! You can follow the same approach with the cute fruits of Korean dogwood, *Cornus kousa*. This is a popular ornamental dogwood tree grown in Seattle with golf ball-sized pinkish red fruits that ripen in September-October. They have a lot of seeds and peels, but the inner fruit is peachy-flavored. Typically, people eat the fruit fresh by sucking it out of the peel, but if you have enough fruit and patience, it makes good jam. You will absolutely want to use a top-quality sieve and strong spoon!

Plum Excitement
(AKA Five Spice-Vanilla Plum Clafoutis)

Seattle is an excellent place to grow Italian prune plums (*Prunus domestica*), so many people have planted the trees and forgotten about them. Once you have your "plum eyes" on, you will be excited to find the trees dropping so much beautiful fruit! Ask your neighbors if you can harvest their fruit— maybe you can thank them later with a bite of this custardy plum dish if you do not mind them suddenly wising up. Italian plums are especially easy to deal with because they can be eaten slightly firm or quite soft and they will not seem to get bugs while they are chilling there in the tree waiting for you. Their flesh doesn't stick to their pit, so they are a snap to slice open, cut up and dehydrate if you like. I will shut up now and say that the below is one of my favorite ways to use fresh plums! Be sure to use the heavy cream— the taste is not as nice when you try to go low fat. Substitute very ripe pears in autumn or (pitted) sour cherries in early summer if you hanker for the dish off-season. Double the five-spice powder if you want!

INGREDIENTS

1 tablespoon soft butter

1 cup heavy cream
½ cup whole milk
2 large eggs
70 grams sugar (50-60 grams if you like things less sweet)
2 tablespoons cornstarch
2 tablespoons all-purpose flour
¼ teaspoon kosher salt
seeds of a 1-inch piece of vanilla bean
½ teaspoon Chinese five-spice powder*

350-400 grams (≈2+ cups) pitted Italian plums, artistically sliced in strips to an equal thinness of about ¼-½ inch
2 tablespoons brown or turbinado sugar

93

DIRECTIONS

Preheat the oven to 350° F and generously coat the bottom of a 9-inch glass or ceramic pie pan with the soft butter.

Whisk together the cream through five spice powder until fully combined, then pour about two thirds of a cup of it into the dish. Bake 12 minutes.

Now add the sliced plums on top of the lightly baked custard in a tidy, even arrangement, sprinkle on the turbinado sugar, and gently pour the rest of the custard mixture over the plums.

Bake for about 50 minutes. If that seems long to you, you can tent aluminum foil over it for the last 10 minutes. When it is done, the custard will be puffy and pleasantly browned. It will still jiggle in the middle. Let it cool to at least "warm" level before consuming, but room temperature is best. It will be soft and yummy, and the center will firm up when it reaches room temperature. Immediately before serving, dust lightly with powdered sugar for extra fanciness.

ITALIAN PLUM MAFIA

Candied Rose Hips

Effortful but worthwhile! Choose meaty rose hips, because you will be scraping seeds out of the final product and you want to be sure there is some substance left at the end. As I say in the Beverages section, please look for rose hips that taste good to begin with! Quite a few varieties are bland, but when you run across the hips that taste good, you will enjoy them! I like *Rosa rubiginosa* in particular.

INGREDIENTS

1 cup white sugar
1 cup water
2 cups ripe, clean rosehips

½ cup white sugar

DIRECTIONS

First make a simple syrup by mixing the water with the sugar. Heat and stir until the sugar dissolves. Add the hips and simmer on medium heat for 10-20 minutes or until the hips are soft—the time required will vary by your type of hips and their stage of ripeness. You may need to add smidges of hot water to the pot as some will evaporate as it gently bubbles away.

When the hips are soft, allow them to cool in the syrup. When completely cool enough to touch, carefully remove from syrup, slice open and remove all seeds with a sharp little spoon. Be *very* thorough about removing the seeds and know that you will get sticky.* Strain the syrup through a fine sieve to make sure there are absolutely no seeds in it, too.

Spread out the hips on a metal cooking rack set over parchment paper to dry overnight or up to 24 hours.

Toss the hips in the remaining granulated sugar, and chop into smaller bits. Toss again in sugar to coat fully. Store in a glass jar.

The hips are nice just as little sweet-sour bites on their own, but I like to use them in ice cream. I make a basic cream gelato and add as many hips as I feel like, chopped, in the last few minutes of churning.

Be sure to keep the rose hip syrup handy for any interesting application you can think of! I recommend it mixed with ice-cold seltzer water, and it is the perfect syrup with which to soak namoura, a delicious Lebanese semolina cake. If you believe that your syrup is too runny, it is OK to heat it on the stove on low to evaporate some water out. And it is OK to add a little water if you want it runnier for some reason. Yum!

Note: You can follow a relatively similar candying procedure with the dried roots of wild ginger, *Asarum caudatum*. I considered including a recipe for that here, but then decided that it is far too rare in the Seattle area to encourage anyone to pick it. But if you have plentiful wild ginger on hand, you can candy it, too. Beware (or rejoice!) that wild ginger roots are said to have a laxative effect.

*Wait! Did you find a variety of rose hips that are easy to seed *before* cooking them? Then by all means seed them before cooking in the syrup and spare yourself the sticky fingers!!

HOLD ME CLOSER, TINY HIPSTERS

Candied Violets

Another item for the "effortful but worthwhile" category! You may choose any edible flower that you think is beautiful and will look nice well-coated with sugar, but my favorite is violets (*Viola spp.*) because you can get them to lie flat fairly easily and they have any interesting shape. I like to use these flowers to top a fancy spring time birthday cake or cupcakes, but you can do anything you want with them!

INGREDIENTS

≈20 violet flowers (or as many as you like)
1 teaspoon meringue powder*
1 tablespoon water
Pinch kosher salt

Superfine white sugar

DIRECTIONS

Have some pieces of parchment paper, a small soft paintbrush, a spoon, and a sharp pair of scissors ready. Stir up the water, meringue powder, and a pinch of salt in a little bowl. Put the sugar in a small bowl.

Pick your flowers, leaving stems intact. Pick them perfectly clean, dry, and dust free because you are not going to be able to wash them! Get back to the kitchen ASAP. Gently hold the flower by its stem down on some parchment and, using the paintbrush, paint both sides gently and thoroughly with the meringue powder mixture. Rest the flower, stem up, in the bowl of sugar, and use the spoon to sprinkle sugar over it. Have a good peak at the flower to see that the sugar is fully coating it. Tap any extra sugar off, gently, then move the flower to a clean piece of parchment, face down. Snip the stem off as close to the flower as you can. Repeat with all flowers. The flowers should ideally dry within a few hours or overnight. You can use the flowers as soon as they are sufficiently stiff and dry.

The word on the street is that if you have completed all steps of the process correctly, the candied flowers will keep for quite a while. I have kept them in a container with layers of parchment paper in between with a silica gel packet in the container to absorb excess moisture, but I have always used them within a few days. If they have been hanging around for a questionable period of time, please look very closely at them for any signs of spoilage.

*Use an actual egg white if you are not concerned about its rawness.

1ST ANNUAL NON-VIOLENT VIOLET COMMUNICATION CONFERENCE

THE WRAP UP

Once again, we have wasted a perfectly good time together, but at least we wasted it traipsing down the foraged plants rabbit hole! If you made it this far and you feel disgruntled because you are wondering where the recipes for the mushrooms and shellfish are located, since those are also technically forageable in our area, look, folks, the sneaky *sub*-subtitle of the book specifies *plants*, not fungi or crustaceans. And for some unfathomable reason, both fungi and crustaceans make me feel more than a little squeamish—with just a few very minor exceptions. So, before I experience any additional undue piloerection, let's not discuss either fungi or shellfish further and leave those topics to other enthusiasts.

Back to plants and wrapping up! Remember that curiosity leads to creativity. Keep an open mind with possible plant substitutions. Work with what you have on hand, and always feel free to make changes that suit your tastes, interests, and intuition. Finally, I will say it once more: abundance is here now—and it is delicious. I wish you yumminess in your future foraged foods experimentations!

TOP SECRET NON-SECRET APPENDIX: ALL PLANTS

Common Name	Latin Name	Parts	Uses	Substitutions	Season
Amaranth	*Amaranthus cruentus*	Leaves	Salad, seeds are a grain	Spinach, arugula, mâche, watercress, other microgreens	Summer
Apple	*Malus domestica*	Fruit	Fruit	Pears, crabapples	Summer-Autumn
Bay laurel	*Umbellularia californica*	Leaves	Seasoning	—	Year round
Bittercress	*Cardamine hirsuta*	Leaves	Salad	Mâche, baby spinach or arugula	Winter
Black nightshade	*Solanum nigrum*	Fruit (be very careful - completely ripe and black)	Fruit or "vegetable"	Cherry tomato	Summer
Blackberry	*Rubus armeniacus*	Leaves, fruits	Beverage, dessert	Any berry such as raspberry	Summer
Blueberries	*Vaccinium*	Fruits	Yumminess	Any small berry, such as huckleberry	Summer
Burdock	*Arctium minus*	Roots	Stir fry vegetable	firm white sweet potato	Summer
Cattail	*Typha latifolia*	Pollen (most parts edible)	Flour for pancakes	Nut meal (hazelnut, almond)	Summer
Chickweed	*Stellaria media*	Leaves	Salad, cooked greens	Mâche, baby spinach or arugula	Autumn-Spring
Chicory	*Cichorium intybus*	leaves, flowers	Cooked greens, salad	Collards, turnip greens, nettles	Spring
Common mallow	*Malva sylvestris*	Leaves, seed pods	Smoothie, cooked greens,	Spinach, kale, nettles, gai lan leaves or chard	Autumn-Spring
Cornelian cherry	*Cornus mas*	Fruits	Beverage, jam	Tart pie cherries	Summer
Crabapples, apples	*Malus domestica*	Fruits	Fruit, snack	Apples	Autumn
Daisy	*Bellis perennis*	Whole flower	Salad decor	Any edible flower	Spring
Daylily	*Hemerocallis fulva*	Flower buds	Stir-fry vegetable	String beans, baby okra, asparagus	Spring-Summer
Dandelion	*Taraxacum officinale*	Leaves, flowers	Salad	Kale, chard, artichokes, broccoli, gai lan or turnip greens	Winter
Douglas fir	*Pseudotsuga menziesii*	New needle growth	Beverage	Citrus peels	Spring

Common Name	Latin Name	Parts	Uses	Substitutions	Season
Dwarf mallow	*Malva neglecta*	Leaves, seed pods	Smoothie, cooked greens	Spinach, kale or chard	Autumn-Spring
Elderberry	*Sambucus canadensis or Sambucus nigra*	Flowers, fruits	Beverage, dessert	No flower substitution, any berry	Spring-Summer
Evergreen huckleberries	*Vaccinium ovatum*	Fruits	Fruit, snack	Blueberries	Autumn-Winter
Fennel	*Foeniculum vulgare*	Flowers, fruits	Spice	Anise	Spring-Autumn
Field bindweed	*Convolvulus arvensis*	Leaves	Cooked greens	Spinach, kale, nettles or chard	Spring
Fig	*Ficus carica*	Leaves, fruits	Cooked greens, fresh fruit	Grape leaves	Spring-Summer
Goumi	*Elaeagnus multiflora*	Fruits	Salad	pomegranate	Summer
Grand fir	*Abies grandis*	New needle growth	Beverage	Citrus peels	Spring
Hawthorn	*Crataegus monogyna*	Fruits (*sans seeds*)	Beverage	Apples, crabapples	Summer-Winter
Hazelnuts	*Corylus cornuta*	Nuts	Various	Almonds	Summer
Hedge bindweed	*Calystegia sepium*	Leaves	Cooked greens	Spinach, kale	Spring
Italian plum	*Prunus domestica*	Fruits	Dessert	Any plum, apricots	Summer
Korean dogwood	*Cornus kousa*	Fruits	Jam, snack	Peaches	Summer
Milk thistle	*Silybum marianum*	Stems, leaves	Salad, general vegetable	Kale, collards for leaves, broccoli or gai lan for stems	Spring
Lamb's quarters	*Chenopodium album*	Leaves	Salad	Mâche, baby spinach, microgreens	Spring
Miner's lettuce	*Claytonia perfoliata*	Leaves	Salad greens	Spinach, arugula, mâche, watercress, other microgreens	Spring
Mint	*Mentha spp.*	Leaves	Salad, seasoning herb	Any cultivated mint	Spring-Autumn
Nasturtium	*Tropaeolum*	Flowers, seed pods	Salad, condiment	Capers, other edible flowers	Summer
Nettle	*Urtica dioica*	Leaves (young ones)	Beverage, cooked greens	Spinach, arugula, mâche, watercress	Spring *and* Autumn

Common Name	Latin Name	Parts	Uses	Substitutions	Season
Ostrich fern	*Matteuccia struthiopteris*	Fiddlehead	Soup, stir-fry	Asparagus (maybe)	Spring
Pineapple weed	*Matricaria discoidea*	Leaves and flowers	Beverage	Actual pineapple?	Spring-Autumn
Plantain	*Plantago lanceolata or Plantago major*	Leaves, flower stems	Salad tidbits	Any greens, green beans, asparagus	Year round
Purslane	*Portulaca oleracea*	Leaves	Salad	Tender, thin-skinned green or wax pepper, raw chopped bok choy stems	Spring-Autumn
Quince	*Cydonia*	Fruits	Savory-sour stew element	Firm pears or apples, but only marginally so	Autumn
Red clover	*Trifolium pratense*	All parts	Salad, soup	Spinach, arugula, mâche, watercress	Spring
Red huckleberries	*Vaccinium parvifolium*	Fruits	Yumminess	Blueberries, wild blueberries	Summer
Rose	*Rosa spp.*	Petals, hips	Beverage, candy	—	Spring-Autumn
Rosemary	*Rosmarinus officinalis*	Leaves, flowers	Seasoning	—	Year round
Salal	*Gaultheria shallon*	Fruits	Yumminess	Blueberries	Summer
Sheep sorrel	*Rumex acetosella*	Leaves	Salad greens	Spinach, arugula, mâche, watercress	Spring *and* Autumn
Sow thistle	*Sonchus oleraceus*	Stems, leaves	Salad	Kale, collards for leaves, broccoli or gai lan for stems	Spring
Violet	*Viola spp.*	Flowers	Candy	Any edible flower	Spring-Summer
Western hemlock	*Tsuga heterophylla*	New needle growth	Beverage	Citrus peels	Spring
White clover	*Trifolium repens*	All parts	Salad, soup	Spinach, arugula, mâche, watercress	Spring
Wild carrot	*Daucus carota*	Flowers	Snack	Carrot	Spring-Summer

Made in the USA
Monee, IL
29 May 2021